Qualitative Researching

JENNIFER MASON

SAGE Publications
London · Thousand Oaks · New Delhi

This edition first published 1996
Reprinted 1997, 1998

SAGE Publications Ltd
6 Bonhill Street
London EC2A 4PU

SAGE Publications Inc
2455 Teller Road
Thousand Oaks, California 91320

SAGE Publications India Pvt Ltd
32, M-Block Market
Greater Kailash – I
New Delhi 110 048

British Library Cataloguing in publication data

A catalogue record for this book is
available from the British Library.

ISBN 0–8039–8985 7
ISBN 0–8039–8986 5 (pbk)

Library of Congress catalog record available

9709090

HM20

Typeset by Type Studio, Scarborough, North Yorkshire
Printed in Great Britain by
Redwood Books, Trowbridge, Wiltshire

CONTENTS

ACKNOWLEDGEMENTS

The impetus to write this book came directly from my experience of teaching postgraduate research students as part of Lancaster University's Social Science Research Training Programme. Between 1990 and 1994 I taught qualitative research methods at introductory and advanced levels to successive groups of research students as part of that programme, and I benefited enormously from the experience. The students were drawn from across the range of social sciences, and one could not have asked for more stimulating, enthusiastic and conscientious course participants. My thinking on qualitative research methods was certainly advanced through our discussions, as I hope was theirs. They are too numerous to name individually, so I should like to record my thanks to all of them. More generally, I have always found research discussions with postgraduate students in seminars, and in supervision sessions, to be very stimulating. In particular, I know my thinking about the challenges and realities of doing social research has been sharpened through lively discussions in seminars I have convened for postgraduate research students in the Department of Applied Social Science at Lancaster University, and more recently in the School of Sociology and Social Policy at Leeds University.

Over the years, I have been fortunate to collaborate with colleagues in the doing of research, as well as the teaching of research methods, and I have also benefited from discussions I have had with other researchers about qualitative methods. I believe that these experiences have made me a better teacher and researcher, and as a consequence have fed in an indirect sense into the writing of this book. In this regard I am grateful to: Rosemary Deem, Caroline Dryden, Janet Finch, Mary Hamilton, Jenny Harris, Lynn Hayes, Sue Heath, Diane Nutt and Lorraine Wallis. In particular I am very privileged to have enjoyed a long and active research collaboration with Janet Finch. It is impossible to track all of the ways in which my qualitative research practice and thinking have benefited from this collaboration. Her exemplary approach to social research, and her intellectual enthusiasm and generosity, continue to be great sources of inspiration to me. I cannot thank her enough.

Andrew Jones read and commented on several of the chapters of the book, and in general the ideas developed here have been sharpened, focused and improved through the many discussions we have had. I am grateful for his clear thinking and for his constant willingness to supply me with constructive comment, intellectual stimulation, encouragement and personal support.

Finally, very special thanks go to my daughter, Rosa Katharine, for her fine sense of timing.

Qualitative
Researching

1

INTRODUCTION: ASKING DIFFICULT QUESTIONS ABOUT QUALITATIVE RESEARCH

My aim in writing this book is to make qualitative research seem *possible* in the eyes of would-be researchers, and to provide them with a set of tools, and a mode of critical thinking, to help them to do it. As an active social researcher myself, as well as a supervisor and tutor to postgraduate researchers, and a teacher of research methodology, I have become increasingly aware that at least two undesirable things can happen when would-be researchers start to engage with methodological issues. The first is that they can become quickly bored with what may seem like endless sets of instructions about methodological technique. The second is that they can become daunted by the more fundamental difficulties involved in actually doing good quality research. In a sense, the first problem arises where technique is addressed without a consideration of the really interesting intellectual and practical challenges of doing research, and the second arises when these challenges come to seem overwhelming. The danger for the research community is that the very people who are likely to become good researchers may be those who are the quickest to perceive, and consequently to feel overwhelmed by, the challenges posed by qualitative research in particular. Either way, whether the would-be qualitative researcher feels daunted by the challenges, or simply bored by the mass of technical advice, the possibility of their actually doing some qualitative research becomes remote.

I think the best way to demonstrate that qualitative research is both interesting and challenging, yet possible, is to focus on the active processes of thinking about it, making decisions about it, and doing it. Any researcher has to identify and resolve a whole range of issues in the research process, most of which are specific in some way to their particular research project, and many of which cannot be anticipated in advance. They therefore need to develop active skills which include identifying the key issues, working out how they might be resolved, and understanding the intellectual, practical, ethical and political implications of different ways of resolving them. I have tried to write a book which will help qualitative researchers to do this, by encouraging them to develop critical yet productive ways of thinking and doing. I should, however, also make it clear at the start what the book does not do.

First of all, it does not provide a blueprint or set of 'recipes' for qualitative research which can simply be followed, and in that sense it is not a book which gives detailed advice simply about research *technique*. This is partly because I think that such a blueprint for qualitative research does not actually exist and cannot usefully be created. More specifically, however, I believe that the passive following of recipes is not a particularly useful skill to encourage in would-be researchers, given my concern with the active recognition and resolution of research issues. Secondly, the book does not contain an abstract discussion of the philosophical underpinnings of qualitative research, because such discussions are not the best way to help people to *do* research. At worst they make any research look like a hopeless compromise of principle. At best they may still give no help to researchers who are struggling with the difficult task of turning their philosophical positions and approaches into concrete research strategies. Qualitative researchers need to be able to think and act strategically in ways which combine intellectual, philosophical, technical and practical concerns rather than compartmentalizing these into separate boxes. I have therefore grounded my discussions of research philosophy firmly within the context of specific research issues and strategies.

The book uses the medium of asking 'difficult questions' about qualitative research to achieve its aims. Each chapter contains its own set of difficult questions, which are focused around the kinds of issues which need to be identified and resolved in relation to the elements of the research process under discussion. The questions are not designed to probe qualitative research in the abstract, or to spell out lists of its advantages and disadvantages. Instead, they are intended literally as a set of questions which qualitative researchers should address to themselves, and answer appropriately, as an active part of the research process. The idea of posing difficult questions is therefore both that they represent a good way to learn about and develop the active 'thinking and doing' skills required for qualitative research, and also that they are an essential component in actually conducting a real piece of research. This means not only that qualitative researchers should ask themselves these kinds of questions in preparation for, or as a training for, research,[1] but also that a major element of their effort during the research process should involve this self-questioning activity. Although it is not possible to anticipate every possible question which any qualitative researcher will need to identify and resolve, and in that sense the questions included in each chapter should not be taken as a definitive checklist, I have focused the questions on some of the most compelling elements of qualitative research. I point out through-out the book that all researchers do, in practice, make decisions in relation to these kinds of questions, and that these decisions have intellectual, practical, ethical and political consequences. It is vital, therefore, that researchers are fully conscious of the decisions they are making, and that these are informed and strategic rather than *ad hoc* or straightforwardly reactive.

WHAT IS QUALITATIVE RESEARCH?

There have been many attempts to define qualitative research in the social sciences, and to determine whether or not it can or should be differentiated from something called quantitative research (see especially Burgess, 1984; Bryman, 1988; Finch, 1986; Hammersley, 1992; Silverman, 1993). However, there is not a consensus on these questions, and we should not be surprised by this, because qualitative research – whatever it might be – certainly does not represent a unified set of techniques or philosophies, and indeed has grown out of a wide range of intellectual and disciplinary traditions.

For example, qualitative research is perhaps most commonly associated with certain schools which fall broadly within what is known as the interpretivist sociological tradition, particularly phenomenology (see for example Schutz, 1976), ethnomethodology (see for example Cicourel, 1964; Garfinkel, 1967) and symbolic interactionism (see for example Blumer, 1969). More recently, postmodernists have begun to show some interest in empirical research and qualitative methods (see Dickens and Fontana, 1994). However, there is also a long anthropological tradition of doing qualitative research, and a more recent interest in the form of discourse analysis from within the discipline of linguistics, which is grounded in the tradition of semiotics (see Fairclough, 1992). Psychology, although long associated with quantitative and 'scientific' research methods, has recently developed a more critical school which favours qualitative approaches to research, particularly those rooted in discourse and content analysis (see Henriques et al., 1984; Henwood and Pidgeon, 1992; Hollway, 1989; Potter and Wetherell, 1987). Other disciplines, such as human geography and education, have conventionally used case study methods, and historians have developed a particular approach to the use of qualitative methods in the writing of oral histories. The 'younger' disciplines of media and cultural studies rely quite heavily on qualitative ways of knowing, as do areas with a strong interdisciplinary bias such as health studies and women's studies. Feminism has indeed had an enormous impact in its challenge to conventional scientific discourse, and in establishing the agenda for a whole range of issues which are now seen as central to qualitative research (see especially Harding, 1986; Rose, 1994; Smith, 1988; Stanley and Wise, 1993).

This is not intended to be a comprehensive list of the influences which have produced what we know as qualitative research, but instead it is meant to convey a sense of the *range* of philosophical underpinnings, as well as methodological techniques and practices, which are likely to be encompassed by the term. These different traditions, schools and disciplines operate with distinctive views about what makes the social world go round, what is important in the social world, what the social world looks like and so on. Consequently they have different ideas about the extent to which empirical research can tell us anything meaningful, and of course about how it might do this. This means that the range of traditions which have some kind of interest in qualitative research do not dovetail neatly into one uniform philosophy or set of methodological principles.

In my view it is a great strength of qualitative research that it cannot be neatly pigeonholed and reduced to a simple and prescriptive set of principles, and I think it is exciting that so many researchers from so many different traditions and disciplines are interested in doing research which is, in some way or another, qualitative in nature. In the chapters which follow, I pose difficult questions which encourage the researcher to identify their own philosophies of research, and to work out how they might in practice conduct research which is consistent with these. I have tried to avoid insisting that there is only one legitimate way of doing qualitative research based on only one philosophical position.

Although I am keen to emphasize the rich variety of qualitative research strategies and techniques, I think it is useful nevertheless to look for some common elements, so that we can develop a sense of what is *qualitative* about qualitative research. However, I wish to go no further than identifying a loose, working definition which says that qualitative research is:

- grounded in a philosophical position which is broadly 'interpretivist' in the sense that it is concerned with how the social world is interpreted, understood, experienced or produced. Whilst different versions of qualitative research might understand or approach these elements in different ways (for example, focusing on social meanings, or interpre- tations, or practices, or discourses, or processes, or constructions) all will see at least some of these as meaningful elements in a complex – possibly multi-layered – social world.

- based on methods of data generation which are flexible and sensitive to the social context in which data are produced (rather than rigidly standardized or structured, or removed from 'real life' or 'natural' social context, as in some forms of experimental method).

- based on methods of analysis and explanation building which involve understandings of complexity, detail and context. Qualitative research aims to produce rounded understandings on the basis of rich, contextual, and detailed data. There is more emphasis on 'holistic' forms of analysis and explanation in this sense, than on charting surface patterns, trends and correlations. Qualitative research usually does use some form of quantification, but statistical forms of analysis are not seen as central.

I do not feel comfortable with specifying any further 'common' features of qualitative research, and the reader will gather in the chapters which follow that there are many different 'qualitative' answers to central questions of methodology. Some of the answers may apply to what is known as 'quantitative' research as well, and I do not think research practice has to involve stark either/or choices between qualitative and quantitative methodology. Partly, this is because neither 'quantitative' nor 'qualitative' methodologies are the unified bodies of philosophy, method and technique which they are sometimes seen to be. This means that any researcher should always think carefully about integrating different methods, whether or not they think they are integrating quantitative with qualitative methods, or qualitative with qualitative, or quantitative with quantitative. The latter two options cannot be assumed to be unproblematic, in my view, any more than the first option should be seen as technically impossible. The key to integrating methods of any description, as I shall argue throughout the book, is to establish what you are trying to achieve in so doing, and to understand the implications of combining approaches which may have different underpinning logics, and which may suggest different forms of analysis and different ways of constructing social explanations.

WHAT SHOULD QUALITATIVE RESEARCH BE?

I have said that I wish not to impose one version of qualitative research upon the reader, but instead to encourage the kind of active engagement with key issues which will help the reader to make their own research decisions. Of course, it would be fair to say that this in itself constitutes an approach to the doing of qualitative research, and I cannot – and would not wish to – claim that I am neutral on all questions of judgement to do with qualitative methodology. On the contrary, I do of course have views on what qualitative research should be, and on what it should do. Indeed, the impetus for writing the book was a concern to encourage skilled researchers to do qualitative research well, because I think such research is highly valuable and important. My ideas about what qualitative research should be are expressed most fully in the kinds of difficult questions I pose in the chapters which follow, and the possibilities which I spell out for answering them. However, I want to preface those chapters with a few key points about what qualitative research can and, in my view, should be.

- Qualitative research should be *systematically and rigorously conducted*. I do not think there are any excuses for a casual or *ad hoc* approach to qualitative research. The difficult questions posed throughout the book are intended to get researchers to think, plan and act in systematic and rigorous ways in the research process. This should, however, be distinguished from a rigid or structured approach, which is usually not appropriate for qualitative research.

- Qualitative research should be *strategically conducted, yet flexible and contextual*. Essentially, this means that qualitative researchers should make decisions on the basis not only of a sound research strategy, but also of a sensitivity to the changing contexts and situations in which the research takes place.

- Qualitative research should involve critical self-scrutiny by the researcher, or active *reflexivity*. This means that the researcher should constantly take stock of their actions and their role in the research process, and subject these to the same critical scrutiny as the rest of their 'data'. This is based on the belief that a researcher cannot be neutral, or objective, or detached, from the knowledge and evidence they are generating. Instead, they should seek to understand their role in that process. Indeed, the very act of posing difficult questions to oneself in the research process is part of the activity of reflexivity.

- Qualitative research should produce social *explanations to intellectual puzzles*. Later on I shall argue that all qualitative research should be formulated around an intellectual puzzle – that is, something which the researcher wishes to explain. I do not think it is sufficient for a researcher to say that they wish simply to describe something, or explore what is happening. Descriptions and explorations involve selective viewing and interpretation; they cannot be neutral, objective or total. The elements which a researcher chooses to see as relevant for a description or exploration will be based, implicitly or explicitly, on a way of seeing the social world, and on a particular form of explanatory logic. What I am advocating is that qualitative researchers recognize that they are producing social explanations, and are explicit about the logics on which these are based.

- Qualitative research should produce social explanations which are *generalizable* in some way, or which have a wider resonance. I do not think qualitative researchers should be satisfied with producing explanations which are idiosyncratic or particular to the limited empirical parameters of their study. This is not to underestimate the challenges posed by generalizing from qualitative – or indeed any – research. These are discussed later in the book.

- Qualitative research should not be seen as a unified body of philosophy and practice, whose methods can simply be combined unproblematically. Similarly, qualitative research should not be seen as necessarily in opposition to, and uncomplementary to, quantitative research. *The distinction between quantitative and qualitative methods is not entirely clear cut*, and all researchers should think very carefully about how and why they might combine any methods, whether qualitative, quantitative, or both.

- Qualitative research should be conducted as *an ethical practice*, and with regard to its political context. Many of the specific ethical and political dilemmas raised by qualitative research are discussed throughout the book.

STRUCTURE AND ORGANIZATION OF THE BOOK

All of the themes and issues which have been raised in this introduction are taken up more fully in subsequent chapters. The chapters are organized around more or less discrete elements of the research process about which decisions need to be made, although I should emphasize that these are not intended to represent sequential stages. Indeed, qualitative research involves moving back and forth between different elements in the research process, and the researcher should not assume that they can deal with only one element at a time.

Chapter 2 deals with questions about planning and designing qualitative research. In particular it examines how researchers might determine what their research is 'really about', and what is its intellectual puzzle. The concepts of 'ontology' and 'epistemology' are introduced in this chapter. These concepts represent different ways of asking what your research is really about, and they are explored in some detail in the chapter. Although ontology and epistemology are often considered to be difficult concepts to grasp, I argue that it is nevertheless very important that researchers do think about their own projects in these terms. The chapter focuses on the centrality of the research question to the research process, and of linking research questions to one's philosophical or methodological position on the one hand, and to appropriate data generation methods on the other. Some of the difficult issues involved in integrating different methods in relation to the same intellectual puzzle are addressed, and finally there is an exploration of some of the ethical and political implications of research design. Overall, the chapter is intended to encourage the reader to develop the necessary skills to produce a qualitative research design. However, given that research design requires knowledge about and planning of all elements in the research process, it cannot really be done properly without a full consideration of the difficult questions raised about these elements in the other chapters.

Chapters 3 and 4 explore some of the main methods for generating qualitative data, as well as investigating questions about what actually constitute data. The chapters engage with ontological, epistemological, practical and ethical issues associated with the different data generation methods. Chapter 3 focuses on qualitative interviewing, whilst Chapter 4 looks at the use of observation, documents and visual data.

Chapter 5 discusses the difficult business of sampling and selecting in qualitative research. It argues that we should not see these activities as associated simply or even primarily with quantitative or statistical modes of sampling. The chapter discusses alternative logics which might underpin qualitative sampling and selection, and emphasizes the link between strategic sampling and consequent analytical and explanatory possibilities. Finally, the reader is invited to engage with a range of difficult questions about the practice of sampling and selection.

Chapters 6 and 7 explore the analytical process, beginning in Chapter 6 with a discussion of a range of techniques for sorting, organizing and indexing qualitative data, and moving on in Chapter 7 to a discussion of how qualitative material might be fashioned into social explanations which are convincing. The chapter suggests that qualitative researchers should work hard to convince first themselves, then others, of the legitimacy of their analyses and explanations. The criteria conventionally used for judging research – namely, reliability or accuracy, validity, and generalizability – are discussed in this context.

Finally, in Chapter 8, the book turns to a discussion of 'the qualitative research practitioner'. This chapter draws together key strands from the book, to discuss the role of the qualitative researcher as a thinking, reflexive, practitioner. The chapter suggests that this role means that qualitative researchers are particularly well placed to contribute to contemporary debates about key issues in social research, and two of these debates are singled out for discussion: ethics and politics in social research, and the integration of different research methods.

NOTE

1 Some readers may wish to use the difficult questions posed in the book as the basis for practical exercises as part of the learning or training process, or as a distance learning resource.

2

PLANNING AND DESIGNING QUALITATIVE RESEARCH

Most social researchers have little difficulty in selecting a broad topic or area for research. They may for example identify a gap in our knowledge of some aspect of the social world, or a set of issues whose exploration seems particularly timely, or a particular substantive interest relating to their own experiences, or they may even be commissioned by an organization to research a particular set of events, or to evaluate a social programme. However, whilst identifying a general interest or topic in this way is fairly straightforward, it is much more of a challenge to design an effective project with a clear, relevant and intellectually worthwhile focus to explore your topic. In this chapter we will address the issues involved – and the difficult questions to ask along the way – in moving from a broad or general research interest, to an effective and workable qualitative research design.

One of the first questions which we should address however is why it is important to produce a research plan or design at all. This question is particularly pertinent because, in the qualitative research tradition, there is a great deal of resistance to the idea that researchers should specify sets of formal hypotheses within a rigid research design at the outset of their research. The resistance comes from an objection to the notion that it is possible or desirable to specify meaningful hypotheses and then to design a project to 'test them out'. Qualitative research is very often seen as having a more fluid and exploratory character than this, which means that an all-encompassing research design cannot necessarily be completed before the research is begun. It is therefore sometimes assumed that the concept of a research design is really only appropriate to quasi-experimental forms of quantitative social research in the positivistic tradition.

However, this is not so. Of course, even if they wanted to, most researchers do not have the luxury of deciding whether or not to produce a research design, because they are required to do so for the consumption of an outside audience such as their funders or 'clients', their supervisors, their peers, research gatekeepers, or those whom they research. The purpose of producing a research design in this context may be to gain or retain funding, support or access, to convince others of the value or intellectual credibility of the research, to demonstrate some form of external accountability, or simply to describe the scope and purpose of the research to those involved. In the 'real world' of social research these are clearly good enough reasons to produce a research design. However, in my view there are also very good

intellectual and practical reasons why qualitative researchers should produce workable research designs, and these reasons are to do with the value
of a good research design for the researcher's own use, and for the coherent
and rigorous development of their project. This chapter will examine the
role of research design, and identify the key issues which researchers should
confront in producing plans and designs for qualitative research. The
chapter is divided into four sections. The first develops the idea that
researchers should be clear about what is the *essence* of their enquiry, and
should express this as an 'intellectual puzzle' with a clearly formulated set of
research questions; the second explores issues involved in linking research
questions, methodologies and methods in qualitative research design; the
third examines some of the ethical concerns which should be addressed in
the design process; and the fourth focuses on the practicalities of actually
producing a research design, in the light of the discussion of the previous
sections.

WHAT IS MY RESEARCH ABOUT? FIVE DIFFICULT QUESTIONS ABOUT THE ESSENCE OF YOUR ENQUIRY

It is well known that researchers who are in the early stages of their work
often find it very difficult to explain to others briefly but specifically what
their research is about. Many can come up with a short but over-general
version, such as 'the experience of disability' or 'gender in the classroom' or
'post-apartheid South Africa'. Alternatively, most researchers can produce
a long and detailed version of their research focus. But the middle course
between these two is often very elusive and the struggle for any researcher,
in my view, is to be able to articulate what is the essence of their enquiry. I
think it is a struggle because, in order to get to this essence, researchers have
to ask themselves some difficult questions, and at the outset of research it
can feel much easier to avoid these. I think there are five of these difficult
questions, and indeed any researcher, whether of a qualitative or quantitative orientation, should address these. Each of the questions is produced
below in a form which is designed to encourage you as a researcher to
interrogate your own assumptions, to systematize them, and possibly to
transform them. Whilst any researcher is unlikely to produce a research
design which provides a clearly formulated set of answers to each of these
five questions, they nevertheless need to *know* what the answers are if they
are going to produce a good, and useful, research design. All five questions
involve asking what your research is about. The first deals with the
fundamental matter of what, according to you as a researcher, constitutes
social reality, as follows.

> What is the nature of the phenomena, or entities, or social 'reality', which I wish to investigate?

This question requires you to ask yourself what your research is about in a fundamental way, and probably involves a great deal more intellectual effort than simply identifying a research topic. Because it is so fundamental, it takes place earlier in the thinking process than the identification of a topic. It involves asking what you see as the very nature and essence of things in the social world, or, in other words, what is your *ontological* position or perspective. Ontology can seem like a difficult concept precisely because the nature and essence of social things seem so fundamental and obvious that it can be hard to see what there is to conceptualize. In particular, it can be quite difficult to grasp the idea that it is possible to have an ontological position or perspective (rather than simply to be familiar with the ontological components of the social world), since this suggests that there may be different versions of the nature and essence of social things. Yet it is only once it is recognized that alternative ontological perspectives might tell different stories that a researcher can begin to see their own ontological view of the social world as a position which should be established and understood, rather than an obvious and universal truth which can be taken for granted. The best way to grasp that you have an ontological position, and to work out what it is and what are its implications for your research, is therefore to recognize what the alternatives are. Let us consider some examples. From different ontological perspectives social reality might be made up of any of the following:

- people, social actors
- bodies, subjects, objects
- minds, psyches
- rationality, emotion, thought, feeling, memory, senses
- consciousness, subconsciousness, instincts
- understandings, interpretations, motivations, ideas
- attitudes, beliefs, views
- identity, essence, being
- self, individuals
- others, collectivities
- representations, cultural or social constructions
- experiences, accounts
- stories, narratives, biographies, evolution, development, progress
- texts, discourses
- words, codes, communications, languages
- actions, reactions, behaviours, events

- interactions, situations, social relations
- social or cultural practices
- social processes
- rules, morality, belief systems
- institutions, structures, the 'material', markets
- cultures, societies, groups, producers, consumers
- nature, genes, humans, animals
- empirical patterns, regularities, order, organization, connectedness
- empirical haphazardness, spontaneity, disorder, disorganization, chaos and disconnectedness
- underlying mechanisms
- one objective reality, multiple realities or versions.

This is not intended to be a complete list of ontological components, but it should help to illustrate the range of possibilities encompassed by the social sciences. You will note that these suggest different versions of the essential or component properties of social reality/ies, and different ideas about where these are located (for example, in individuals' heads, in social, legal or administrative structures). There are of course also different versions of whether and how these things relate or connect up in social life. You will recognize some of these ways of conceptualizing social entities, and may be able to connect them with different philosophies of social science. This should alert you to the possibility that different versions of ontology may be logically competing rather than complementary, so that you cannot simply pick and choose bits of one and bits of another in an eclectic or *ad hoc* way. Some of the properties in the list above, and the distinctions between them, are actively disputed and contested by opposing perspectives in the social sciences. So, for example, whether or not it is possible or meaningful to distinguish between: subject and object; mind and body; rationality, emotion, thought and feeling; nature and culture; action and interpretation; have been the subjects of long running disputes between positivists, relativists, feminists, realists, and so on. Some of the properties listed may appear more well matched with qualitative research methodology than others – for example, social processes, interpretations, social relations, social practices, experiences, understandings, seem particularly well matched. Some gain more credence in the conventions of some social science disciplines than others (see Chapter 7 for a further discussion of this; see also Blaikie, 1993; Stanley and Wise, 1993). You therefore need to understand the implications of adopting a particular version or set of versions of ontology.

Some researchers may feel unable to answer these ontological questions fully at the beginning of their research. Possibly this will be because they wish the research to address these very issues rather than simply to start from them, or even to attempt to adjudicate between some of the disputed distinctions. However, if that is so then it must be an explicit aim, formulated through research questions, since more often a reluctance to address these issues stems from vagueness, imprecision, or a failure to understand that there is more than one ontological perspective.

The second question invites you to think about what your research is about in a different way.

> What might represent knowledge or evidence of the entities or social 'reality' which I wish to investigate?

Questions about what we regard as knowledge or evidence of things in the social world are *epistemological* questions and, overall, this second question is designed to help you to explore what kind of epistemological position your research expresses or implements. It is important to distinguish questions about the nature of evidence and knowledge – epistemological questions – from what are apparently more straightforward questions about how to collect, or what I shall call 'generate', data (see Chapter 3). Your epistemology is, literally, your theory of knowledge, and should therefore concern the principles and rules by which you decide whether and how social phenomena can be known, and how knowledge can be demonstrated. Epistemological questions should therefore direct you to a consideration of philosophical issues involved in working out exactly what you would count as evidence or knowledge of social things. You should be able to connect the answers to these questions with your answers to the ontological questions, and the two sets of answers should be consistent so that, for example, your epistemology helps you to generate knowledge and explanations about the ontological components of the social world, be they social processes, social actions, discourses, meanings, or whatever, which you have identified as central (see Chapter 7 for a discussion of the construction of explanations). There may be lots of possibilities and, again, therefore the researcher must recognize not only that there is more than one epistemology, but also that they will not all be complementary or equally consistent with their own ontological position. Again, some epistemologies may appear to be more consistent with a qualitative methodology than others, or have greater credibility within certain social science disciplines than in others.

The third question looks a little like the starting point for a research project, but should actually follow from your answers to the first and second questions.

> What topic, or broad substantive area, is the research concerned with?

Although this appears to be the all-encompassing question about your broad research interest or topic, and is certainly the one which preoccupies most researchers in the early stages of their work, I want to suggest that the answer must follow from your answers to the ontological and epistemological questions above. Usually a research topic will express something of the researcher's ontological or epistemological position. For example, let us take the topic of racism. Using the concept of racism itself suggests that the social world is in some way or other organized around whatever racism is defined to be, and that this is knowable, or can be made knowable, through social research. If we move a little closer to a more clearly defined research topic, the ontological and epistemological dimensions become clearer. So, for example, a study of racist attitudes amongst school children would at the very least suggest an ontological position which says that individual people (children) hold attitudes, and that those attitudes are meaningful components of the social world. We might contrast that with a study which focuses on institutional racism within schools, or racist actions within classrooms, or racist discourse. The first of these might suggest an ontological position which sees institutions, collectivities or structures, rather than (or as well as) individuals, as meaningful components of the social world. The second might suggest a position which sees actions, but not necessarily attitudes, as meaningful. The third might suggest a position which sees neither individuals, nor institutions, as meaningful, but instead sees cultural texts or 'scripts' as core components of the social world. In terms of epistemology, each of these different research topics is suggesting that distinctive dimensions of the social world (for example, attitudes, actions, discourses) are knowable – that it is possible to generate knowledge about and evidence for them. The topics themselves tell us little more about what form each of these epistemologies might take, but at the very least we would know that a study designed to explore racist attitudes, which goes on to encompass an epistemology stating that only texts and discourses are knowable, has some major and possibly irreconcilable inconsistencies.

The fourth question is:

> What is the intellectual puzzle? What
> do I wish to explain? What are my
> research questions?

Again, the answer to this question must connect with the other three. In answering this question you should be addressing yourself to the intellectual and theoretical contributions of your work. Not all researchers will see their projects as 'theoretical' but, as I suggested in Chapter 1, in my view all qualitative research should be constructed around an intellectual puzzle of some kind, and should attempt to produce some kind of explanation of that puzzle. Intellectual puzzles can and do take a variety of forms connected to the ontological and epistemological positions encapsulated in the research, and grounded within the specific context of their research problem. It is also the case that different theoretical and intellectual traditions in the social sciences are preoccupied with different kinds of intellectual puzzle, and consequently different kinds of social explanation. There is a fuller discussion of these issues in Chapter 7 where we explore the construction of social explanations, but for now some examples of three common yet distinctive types of puzzle will help to make the point. You might, for example, pose a developmental puzzle – how and why did x or y develop? The x or y might be anything, ontologically speaking, for example racist attitudes, cultural imperialism, the American system of government, a mental illness, and so on. You might, alternatively, pose a mechanical puzzle – how does x or y work? Why does it work in this way? Again, x or y might be anything – intimate personal relationships, a legal system, a penal institution, the human psyche, and so on. Or you might pose a causal puzzle – what influence does x have on y, or what causes x or y?

Intellectual puzzles, then, will contain different sets of ontological and epistemological assumptions and prescriptions, and will suggest distinctive types of social explanation. In formulating your own intellectual puzzle, you must ensure that you have thought through what these are, and be confident that they are consistent – that is, that your puzzle is ontologically meaningful, and epistemologically explainable or workable.

One of the main virtues of expressing whatever it is you want to research and explain as a puzzle is that it focuses your mind on *research questions*. Once you are thinking in terms of puzzles and explanations, it will be a relatively easy task to formulate a set of research questions, and these will form the backbone of your research design. I use the term 'research question' in preference to, for example, 'hypothesis' or 'proposition', partly because qualitative approaches usually entail formulating questions to be explored and developed in the research process, rather than hypotheses to be tested by or against empirical research. But also, the concept of research question fits generally with a wider range of ontological and epistemological positions than do these other terms. A research question is a question which the research is designed to address (rather than, for example, a question which an interviewer might ask an interviewee) and, taken together, your research questions should express the essence of your enquiry. Therefore, you need to have done a great deal of thinking about the essence of your enquiry in the sense of its ontology, its epistemology, and most importantly its intellectual puzzle, in order to be able to formulate research questions sensibly and coherently. They should be clearly formulated (whether or not you intend to modify them or add to them later), intellectually worthwhile, and researchable (both in terms of your epistemological position, and in practical terms), because it is through them that you will be connecting what it is that you wish to research with how you are going to go about researching it. They are vehicles which you will rely upon to move you from your broad research interest to your specific research focus and project, and therefore their importance cannot be overstated.

Research questions, then, are those questions to which you as researcher really want to know the answers, and in that sense they are the formal expression of your intellectual puzzle. Although you will formulate them as questions, you may not expect a straightforward answer so much as an opening up of avenues of enquiry to which you will be able to apply analytical reasoning. Their relevance to each other will be ensured because you have thought hard about the logical links between them, and because they are grounded in the essence of your enquiry. The question format will help you to design a study which is focused rather than vague, but which can nevertheless be exploratory and fluid. You should be sure that your questions are formulated in such a way that intellectually interesting answers are possible and probable. So, for example, you will want to avoid questions which would be interesting if answered in the affirmative, but uninteresting if in the negative, or those which hinge your whole project on only one potential answer. With both of these, if you get the 'wrong' answer your research is in serious trouble. You should also use your questions to problematize links between your own and other research and theoretical scholarship in your broad research area, and this is of course one way of ensuring that you are posing intellectually interesting and relevant questions, and not duplicating effort which has already been made elsewhere. Finally, you are likely to want to produce questions of varying types, orders and levels. For example, some may express links between your own and existing work very directly, others indirectly; some may be overarching questions (possibly *the* research question), others smaller sub-questions; and so on.

Here are some examples of research questions used in one of my own research projects.[1] The broad research topic was 'Inheritance, Property and Family Relationships'.

- How is inheritance handled in 'ordinary families' in contemporary Britain?

- What kinds of ideas, norms and beliefs operate in contemporary families concerning the distribution of assets?

- How are matters related to inheritance negotiated, and how do these negotiations link with other family responsibilities and relationships?

- What is the interface between families and the law on matters related to inheritance?

- In relation to all of the above, is there an underlying tension between family responsibilities and the legal principle of testamentary freedom?

As well as illustrating different levels of research question (for example, the first question is very general whereas the subsequent questions are a little more focused and specific), you will note that the way in which the questions are phrased gives away certain ontological and epistemological clues. For example, concepts such as 'ideas', 'norms', 'beliefs', 'negotiations', 'interface between families and the law' give some indications as to the researcher's views about what are meaningful and knowable components of the social world, as well as about how that world can be explained.

Initially, I think it is worth getting yourself fully into the habit of producing research questions by allowing yourself to generate a long list of them. However, as I shall suggest shortly, you will need to modify your list subsequently when you begin to consider how to link your research questions with your methodology and your research methods, and when you start to tackle practical, ethical and political questions. For the time being though, let us continue to focus on the unbridled generation of research questions. To ensure you are on the right track, here are some supplementary questions to ask yourself when formulating your own research questions.

- Am I clear about what is the essence of my enquiry, and my intellectual puzzle? Do my research questions express or problematize these? Are they consistent with them?

- Are my research questions consistent with each other, and linked to each other? Do they add up to a sensible whole?

- Are my research questions coherent? Would anyone but me understand them?

- Do my research questions make possible, and probable, intellectually interesting answers?

- Are my research questions open enough to allow for the degree of exploratory enquiry I require? Will they allow me to generate further questions at a later stage, in the light of my developing data analysis, should I wish?

- Are my questions original and worth asking?

- Am I asking the right number of research questions at this stage?

Of course, as the last question above implies, and as I have already suggested, you will not be producing your research questions in a vacuum, away from the practicalities and indeed the ethics of what you can feasibly do, and the methods available to you to do it. In a moment we will discuss what is involved in linking your research questions with your methodology and your research methods. But first, let us consider the last of the five difficult questions designed to help you to work out what your research is really about.

> What is the purpose of my research?
> What am I doing it for?

In the simplest terms the question is, 'what is my research for?', and I think all researchers should be fully aware of their particular range of answers to it. In thinking about answering this question you should consider not only familiar academic arguments about increasing or challenging intellectual and theoretical understanding, plugging gaps in knowledge, extending debate and so on, but also issues about the socio-political context of your research practice. There is likely to be more than one purpose to any research project, and the different parties involved may have divergent interests in the research. In formulating your answers to this question, you should not overlook what are sometimes unstated purposes like the achievement of social and political change or a contribution to some wider political effort, or personal advancement (for example through access to a higher degree, through the acquisition of research funds). In addition, researchers need to ask questions about the socio-political context of research directly, and understand debates about, for example, the usefulness or emancipatory potential of research. By advocating that researchers think about these issues I am arguing that you should confront and engage with the politics of social research rather than assume it is possible to maintain a safe distance.

Taken together, these five difficult questions represent what I think is a rigorous way to help you to establish what your research is about. Researchers working within and across social science disciplines will come up with many different answers. Indeed, whether you are intending to work within the boundaries of a specific social science discipline, or across boundaries, you will inevitably need to engage with the ways in which different disciplinary conventions would answer these questions. My purpose is not (and cannot be) to tell you what your answers should be, or which disciplinary conventions are the best, but instead to argue that working out a set of answers which are consistent with each other, and understanding the implications of those answers, is a vital part of your research practice. To put it simply, in order to be able to produce a set of research questions – which I am suggesting is essential in a good research design – you will need to know where you stand on these five key issues. After all, that you are contemplating an empirical project at all suggests that you are working within a certain view of the social world (ontology) and how to generate knowledge of it (epistemology) which can be contrasted with the anti-empirical production of abstract, formalized explanations and knowledge.

DO I HAVE A COHERENT RESEARCH STRATEGY? LINKING RESEARCH QUESTIONS, METHODOLOGIES AND METHODS

Your intellectual puzzle and the research questions which express it represent a large part of your overall research strategy or methodology. However, as yet we have not really engaged with the question of research method, which usually refers to data generation techniques and procedures, the selection of data 'sources', and sampling (these are discussed fully in Chapters 3, 4 and 5). The key tasks at the research design stage in relation to method are not only to decide upon appropriate methods and data sources, but also to develop some understanding of the methodological implications of your choices, and in particular to think carefully about the links between your research questions and your research methods. This means being clear about how and why a particular method and data source are going to help you to address your research questions rather than assuming that, for example, a series of unstructured interviews, or some documentary analysis, will obviously and unproblematically tell you what you want to know. In linking your research questions, and your methodology, with a specific set of research methods and techniques, you will need to work out in some detail what might constitute knowledge or evidence relevant to your intellectual puzzle and research questions. You will also need to begin to engage with the question of how you might go about generating and assembling such knowledge and evidence.

Most researchers begin their projects with a better knowledge of and expertise in some data generation techniques and data sources than others, or with implicit or explicit preferences. Whilst these preferences may be appropriate to the research being designed, they may equally be less to do with this than with idiosyncratic factors in the biography of the researcher (for example, that you happen to have been trained in some techniques and not others). Whilst practical issues to do with training and skill are of course relevant in your choice of method (these are discussed later in the chapter), they should not govern your choices at this stage. It is true that some forms of research, for example historical documentary research, may begin with an assessment of what sources or methods are literally available and, in these cases, it is necessary to work backwards towards the intellectual puzzle (see Chapter 4 for a further discussion). However, I think it is nevertheless a good idea, whatever you think are your practical constraints, to begin by consciously trying to broaden your horizons through thinking as widely and creatively as you can about possible relevant sources of data, and methods of selecting and generating them. Your thinking will, of course, be informed by your responses to the five key questions about the essence of your enquiry so that, for example, what you see as a potential data source, or what you see as a method of generating data, will both depend upon and express your ontological and epistemological positions. At this stage, however, it is better to see these positions as enabling rather than constraining, since the object of the exercise initially at least is to think as creatively as you can about data sources and method and, quite possibly, to generate a fairly long list of possible options, which you will go on to modify. Indeed, the activity of generating and modifying such a list can, in itself, help you to firm up on precisely what it is you see as the essence of your enquiry in ontological and epistemological terms. This is because the process of deciding that certain methods are ontologically and epistemologically *in*appropriate can help you to see more clearly what *is* appropriate.

Literally making a list or a chart of possible research method and data source options – including those which you are going to reject – can actually be quite a good way of disciplining yourself systematically to consider all possible options as thoroughly as you can. Talking your list or chart through with a colleague or adviser can be an even better way of broadening your horizons and helping you to see other possibilities, as well as helping you to make choices in a considered way. Whether or not you make a list or chart, you should ask yourself a number of questions about your method and sources. If you are making a chart, you can incorporate these into it by using each question as a heading, and working out the relevant answers for each of the methods and sources you consider. Initially, you will want to consider the following questions:

> What data sources and methods of data generation are potentially available or appropriate?

> What can these methods and sources feasibly tell me about? Which phenomena and components or properties of social 'reality' might these data sources and methods potentially help me to address (ontologically)?

> How or on what basis do I think they could do this (epistemologically)?

> Which of my research questions
> could they help me to address?

Figure 2.1 provides a worked example of a chart which incorporates features identified in these questions. It is based on the research questions used in the research project on 'Inheritance, Property and Family Relationships' which I outlined earlier in the chapter.

Constructing a chart such as this, or asking questions such as these, will help you to begin the process of making choices of method and data source. It will help you to spot and eradicate inconsistencies between, for example, what you think a particular method can yield and what kinds of data you think you need to generate to address your research questions. You can also add corresponding columns to your chart on 'practicalities' (for example, resources, skills required, whether or not you can gain access to the data sources), and 'ethical issues', both of which factors will influence your choice of method. These are discussed shortly. Figure 2.2 shows how they might be incorporated into your chart, to ensure that you are linking your thinking on practicalities and ethics directly with your choice of methods.

Charts such as these provide a fairly simple check on the consistency of your thinking at an early stage in the research process, and will help you to make certain fundamental choices. There are, however, a number of important issues which are not incorporated into the chart, but over which you will have to deliberate, including decisions about sampling, and how many interviews to conduct or documents to analyse, or whatever (sampling is discussed fully in Chapter 5). You will also need to engage with questions concerning how well these methods and sources address your research questions, and what kinds of claims they will potentially enable you to make. I am suggesting not that you have to guess at what your 'findings' are going to be, but instead that you should be beginning to develop your thinking on how – according to what principles and logic – you will formulate explanations and substantiate your claims and your analysis. This means that you should consider how and whether you are going to achieve *validity*, *generalizability* and *reliability*, with these methods and sources, in relation to the research questions as you have posed them. These issues are discussed more fully in subsequent chapters, but they are raised here because they are aspects of your analytical and explanatory logic which must guide you in selecting data sources, methods and combinations of these, in working out what procedures to use in generating your data (see Chapters 3 and 4 for a full discussion), and in deciding upon the principles to use in sampling and selecting (see Chapter 5 for a full discussion). Essentially, validity, generalizability and reliability are different kinds of measures of the quality, rigour and wider potential of research, which are achieved according to certain methodological and disciplinary conventions and principles (see Chapter 7 for a full discussion). It is too late to begin to think about them

Research questions	Data sources and methods	Justification
1 How is inheritance handled in 'ordinary families' in contemporary Britain?	• Family members: interviews Also possibly: • Probated wills: documentary analysis • Solicitors and other professionals: interviews	• Interviews will provide family members' accounts of how they and their relatives have handled inheritance, i.e. based on their own experiences • Analysis of probated wills will reveal how testators' wishes get formally and legally expressed and transacted • Interviews with professionals who handle inheritance will provide their accounts of how family members handle inheritance, i.e. based on their own experiences of dealing with clients
2 What kinds of ideas, norms and beliefs operate in contemporary families concerning the distribution of assets?	• Family members: interviews Also possibly: • Solicitors and other professionals: interviews	• Interviews providing family members' accounts and reported experiences, and their judgements about those experiences, will reveal something of the kinds of ideas, norms and beliefs they and their relatives operate with in relation to inheritance. From this we should be able to discern whether people have ideas about appropriate behaviour • Interviews with solicitors may provide data on these issues, because they will have experiences of dealing with clients who may or may not express such ideas, norms and beliefs
3 How are matters related to inheritance negotiated, and how do these negotiations link with other family responsibilities and relationships?	• Family members: interviews	• The accounts and experiences reported by family members will reveal something of how they came to negotiate their own inheritance experiences. Interviews with more than one member of each family will provide data on different individuals' versions of, and positions within, this negotiating process

	Also possibly: • Solicitors and other professionals: interviews	• Interviews with professionals may provide data on negotiations between family members (these may be reported to professionals, or actually take place during consultations with professionals)
4 What is the interface between families and the law on matters related to inheritance?	• Probated wills: documentary analysis • Solicitors and other professionals: Interviews • Family members: interviews • Legal documents, statutes and precedent: documentary analysis	• Wills provide data on the formal expression of testators' wishes, but also tell us something about the influence of the law on those wishes • Interviews with professionals reveal something of the negotiations taking place between what testators want to do, and what the law will allow them to do. The experience and accounts of professionals should also yield data on their own mediating or negotiating role in this process • Interviews with family members will tell us something about their knowledge of and experience of the law, professional advice on will making, and so on • Documentary analysis of the law and precedent will yield data on the formal and administrative regulation of inheritance, interpretation of testators' wishes, adjudication in family disputes about inheritance, and so on.
5 Is there an underlying tension between family responsibilities and the legal principle of testamentary freedom?	• All methods used in the study	• A comparison of similarities and differences between the data yielded from the different sources will help us to build up a picture of whether or not there is a 'fit' between the law and operation of family responsibilities

1 Based on the research project 'Inheritance, Property and Family Relationships' (see note 1 to chapter).

Figure 2.2   *Chart layout for linking research questions, methods, practicalities and ethics*

Research questions	Data sources and methods	Justification	Practicalities (eg resources, access, skills)	Ethical issues

near the end of the research process, since they need to be influencing decisions you make throughout.

Briefly, if your research is *valid*, this means that you are observing, identifying, or 'measuring' what you say you are. So, in my example of research into inheritance, we would need to be able to show that our data on and analysis of, for example, ideas, norms and negotiations about inheritance, really did relate to these concepts. Validity is often associated with the 'operationalization' of concepts, a term more commonly associated with quantitative and experimental forms of research, but nevertheless one which encapsulates the idea that you need to be able to work out, and to demonstrate, that your concepts can be identified, observed, or 'measured' in the way you say they can. You therefore need to work out how well a particular method and data source might illuminate your concepts, whatever they are.

Generalizability involves the extent to which you can make some form of wider claim on the basis of your research and analysis, rather than simply stating that your analysis is entirely idiosyncratic and particular. There is a variety of ways in which generalizations can be made, using different sets of principles and logic, and these are discussed in Chapter 7. For now you will need to ensure that you are thinking about on what basis, if any, you can make general claims, and about what kinds of general claims your research questions might imply. For example, do you wish to make claims which can be applied to whole populations, empirically? Do you wish to make claims which have a wider theoretical resonance? These may or may not be based on how representative, in empirical terms, your sample is. Will your research questions be meaningfully answered if you cannot make the kinds of claims which are implied?

Finally, *reliability* involves the accuracy of your research methods and techniques. How reliably and accurately do they produce data? How can you maximize their reliability? Research in the quantitative tradition often relies upon standardization of research 'instruments' or 'tools', and upon cross-checking the data yielded by such standardized instruments – and by different sets of instruments which are designed to 'measure' the same thing

– in order to check reliability. Qualitative researchers, as we shall see in subsequent chapters, are highly sceptical of the value or feasibility of such standardization, and indeed of the very concept of research instruments (implying as it does that such instruments can be neutrally applied), but do nevertheless have to think carefully about the reliability and accuracy of their methods.

In fact you are quite likely to want to build up an analysis using data derived from different sources, and generated using different methods, although your main aim in this is unlikely to be to augment the reliability of your study. Instead, it may be because your research questions can be approached from a variety of angles or conceptualized in a variety of ways, suggesting a number of possibilities of method and source, as with the example of the research on inheritance which I gave earlier. It may be because each research question suggests its own distinctive method and source. Or it may be because you want to use different methods or sources to corroborate each other so that you are using some form of methodological 'triangulation' (Denzin, 1989; see also Chapters 4, 7 and 8 for discussions of the use of multiple methods, and of triangulation). Whatever the reason, you will need to think through the implications of using data from different sources, and integrating different methods, for your overall research design and for the strength, validity, generalizability and reliability of the argument you will wish to construct. The integration of different methods is not straightforward. Here are some difficult questions you should ask yourself:

> What am I trying to achieve in integrating data and method?

Are you, for example:

- exploring different parts of a process or phenomenon? If so, you are going to have to work out how the parts are linked. Is this an empirical question which you can answer through data analysis?

- answering different research questions with different methods and sources (or addressing different levels ontologically)? Again, if you are doing this, you will need to work out how to link the different levels.

- answering the same research questions but in different ways or from different angles? Again, you will need to work out how to integrate the different angles.

- wishing to analyse something in greater and lesser depth or breadth, and using different methods accordingly?

- seeking to corroborate one source and method with another, or enhance validity and reliability through some form of triangulation of method? If you are doing this, you will need to think about on what basis one set of data, or one method, can corroborate another. This will involve asking whether the two sets of data tell you about the same phenomena, or whether the two methods yield comparable data. Often they do not, and you cannot therefore expect straightforward corroboration (see Mason, 1994; see also Fielding and Fielding, 1986, for a useful discussion).

- testing different analyses, explanations or theories against each other? This might involve building a study which is designed to test out the validity of different ontological perspectives, for example. That might mean that you conceptualize the social entities under scrutiny in more than one way, and link these up with different sets of data generation methods. If this is your aim, you will need to ensure that you have included the appropriate range of methods and data sources to conduct such a test.

Although these questions are difficult to answer at the research design stage, it is vital that they are addressed. If they are not, the researcher risks assembling an untidy bag of methods with little logic, and with little hope of sensibly integrating the products into a coherent analysis. As well as needing to know why you wish to integrate data and method, you will need to think about the basis on which you intend to do this.

> How – according to what logic – do I expect to be able to add the products together, or to integrate them?

You may not be adding like with like, so you will need to ask yourself whether it is possible to integrate them:

- technically. Do they take a similar or complementary form in a technical or organizational sense, so that they can be straightforwardly aggregated, or grouped together, or made comparable in some way? The answer to this is probably no, because unless different data sets and types of data take an almost identical form, the task of integration is always likely to be a more than technical one. One way of viewing this is to ask whether your different forms of data will use the same, or complementary, 'units of analysis'. For example, if you have conducted qualitative interviews with a sample of people, your unit of analysis might be the individual (although, as we discuss in Chapter 5, your analytical units do not have to mirror exactly the units you use for sampling purposes). This will mean not only that you use the data you generate to tell you something about individuals, but also that aggregations and comparisons which you might make are likely to be aggregations of individuals, and comparisons between individuals. However, you might also have conducted observational studies of particular social settings and your unit of analysis in these cases might be the settings themselves. You cannot, therefore, simply add these different data sets together because their substance and form are fundamentally different, and this means that integrating them is more than just a technical job. You will need to work out how to combine or integrate data which are organized around different analytical units, in this case individuals on the one hand, and social settings on the other. Sometimes of course the analytical unit may be the same in different data sets, but the data may nevertheless take a different form. So, for example, you might wish to integrate data from a structured interview survey with data from loosely structured qualitative interviews. The structured data will probably take a standardized form, and may well be coded or categorized numerically. The unstructured data may be coded thematically. Both sets of codes may use the individual as the analytical unit, but you will need to work out a meaningful basis on which they can be combined, rather than seeing integration as a purely technical task. All of these questions need resolving as well as the more obvious questions about whether different data sets provide data on, for example, literally the same individuals, or the same social settings, and so on. In fact, in most cases the integration of different sets or forms of data is more than a simple technical task, and requires that other issues be resolved.

- ontologically. Are they ontologically consistent? In other words, are they based on similar, complementary or comparable assumptions about the nature of social entities and phenomena? For example, data concerning social discourses or the discursive construction of social life (perhaps a study of the construction of social categories in legal or administrative texts) might be ontologically inconsistent with data concerning individual psyches or personalities. The former may be based on an ontological position which sees social life as a collection of social discourses, and indeed may see the very idea of an individual psyche or personality as a discursive construction rather than empirical reality. Conversely, the latter may be based on a position which sees individual personalities as empirical realities, and social life as a collection of these, or as an arena in which they are played out. From this perspective, social discourses may not be recognized as empirical realities. Seen in this way, these two different perspectives are competing rather than complementary, and data generated in relation to each are unlikely to be easily made compatible. To make them compatible, the researcher needs to work out how – if at all – personalities and discourses might be related in their view of how the social world operates. Their answer might indeed be that personalities are simply discursive constructions, or that discourses are the products of individuals who have motives, personalities and psyches. The point about both of these answers is that they suggest a theory (a different one in each case) of a relationship between discourse and personality, and it is this theory which should underpin the integration method and data in such a study.

- epistemologically, in the sense of what counts as knowledge and as evidence. Do the different methods or forms of data emanate from the same epistemology, or at least from complementary epistemologies? In other words, are they based on similar, complementary or comparable assumptions about what can legitimately constitute knowledge or evidence? For example, in our study of discourse and personality, can the same rules of evidence and knowledge be applied to each element? A study of personality and psyche might, for example, use individual testimonies or observations of behaviour on the basis that these are the best available ways of trying to find out what is going on inside people's heads. A study of discourse might be based on the assumption that we cannot know what is going on inside people's heads and, even if we could, this would not tell us anything very meaningful about social life. Instead, such a study might use documentary data such as laws and statutes, on the basis that these are the best available ways of tracking legal and social discourses. Therefore, the one may see individual testimonies, and the other may see the scrutiny of documentary data, as inherently unreliable or partial forms of method and evidence.

- epistemologically, in terms of the construction of social explanations, and the making of generalizations. Can your different data sources and methods usefully contribute to some kind of coherent explanation of your intellectual puzzle? They may suggest and support different forms of general claim (for example, some may be based on the notion of empirical generalization to a wider population, some on wider theoretical resonance), or they may feed into different ideas about how you can construct an explanation. Can these be brought together meaningfully in a unified explanation? Do they need to be? (A full discussion of different ways of constructing social explanations is contained in Chapter 7.)

These are very difficult questions, and the discussions contained in subsequent chapters should help you to answer them. For example, technical questions about integrating data relate to issues of sampling discussed in Chapter 5, and the organization and indexing of data discussed in Chapter 6. Epistemological and ontological questions about what the social world is made up of, what counts as data and evidence, and how explanations can be constructed, involve methods of data generation discussed in Chapters 3 and 4, and the construction of convincing explanations discussed in Chapter 7. Although the bulk of these discussions cannot be pre-empted, it is essential at this stage to realize that the questions outlined above do form part of the decision making process which goes into designing and planning a research project, so that they cannot be entirely shelved until a later stage in the research process. At the very least, in terms of the integration of different methods and data, you will need to be asking yourself from the beginning what steps you need to take in designing your research to ensure that the kind of integration you seek is possible (see Mason, 1994).

IS MY ENQUIRY ETHICAL? ETHICS, MORALITY AND POLITICS IN QUALITATIVE RESEARCH DESIGN

In my view, ethical concerns must be high on the research design agenda of any researcher. We should be as concerned to produce an ethical research design as we are to produce an intellectually coherent and compelling one. This means attempting not only to carry out our data generation and analysis in an ethical manner (which is discussed more fully in later chapters), but also to begin by framing ethical research questions. Of course this is easier said than done, because however the research questions are framed, any research project is likely to involve a range of interests, some of which may be competing. Therefore the idea that there is one ethical or moral route which is equally fair to all concerned may sound good in theory, but be elusive in practice.

I think it is because of the complexities of research ethics, and because there is unlikely ever to be one clear ethical solution, that a practical approach to ethics which involves asking yourself difficult questions – and pushing yourself hard to answer them – is particularly appropriate. Here are some of the questions which I think are pertinent at the research design stage, when you are formulating your research questions:

> What is the purpose or are the purposes of the research?

We have already asked this question in our pursuit of the essence of your enquiry, but I think it is vital to ask this again with ethics, morals and politics at the forefront of your mind. You may need to push yourself quite hard to be honest about the purpose of your research. It is likely to include not just the advancement of knowledge and understanding, but also factors to do with personal gain such as the achievement of a higher degree, of a promotion, of some standing in your discipline (amongst colleagues, friends, rivals, relatives, and so on), of some research funding. It is part of the politics of research that you should engage with this wider context in which your research is being done. Your research may have explicitly moral or political purposes. You may wish to advance the interests of a particular group through it, or to gain acceptance for some particular form of social organization, or to expose some form of immoral social organization or activity, and so on. This does not necessarily make the ethics of your research more straightforward however, not least because 'the interests of a particular group' may be diverse or contested. The notion of one moral route may therefore still be elusive.

> Which parties, bodies, practices, or whatever, are potentially interested or involved in or affected by this research?

Your answers to the first question should lead you to the conclusion that this might be a fairly wide group, for example, yourself as researcher, your supervisor, your institution, your commissioning body, the people or bodies you research, people who are connected with your data sources in some way, people not directly researched but about whom conclusions may be reached, or generalizations made.

> What are the implications for these parties, bodies, practices, and so on, of framing these particular research questions?

Your answers to these questions will not tell you, of course, whether your research questions are ethical or not, but they will guide you towards identifying the potentially complex range of interests touched upon by your research. If you are explicit about these interests, you can begin to work out which courses of action seem the most reasonable and ethical, and which do not – an activity which you will engage in throughout the research process as you face new situations, contexts and choices. You should think about the sources of your criteria for judging what is moral or ethical, and recognize that these sources are unlikely to be neutral and apolitical. You might, for example, be drawing upon:

- your own experience, values and politics (which are of course likely to be derived from a variety of sources)

- a particular political position on ethics, for example feminist ethics, socialist ethics

- your professional culture, and the norms of acceptability which appear to operate in your professional setting

- codes of ethical practice, which are often developed by a professional body, or within a professional culture

- a legal framework, for example concerning rights of privacy, rights to information, data protection legislation and so on.

It is easy, in the face of a moral research dilemma, to select the least stringent set of moral criteria and to argue that, because one's research questions do not infringe these criteria, they are ethical. Some commentators are unenthusiastic about professional moral codes of conduct precisely because they can be used in this way even though they have usually been written simply to establish a basic minimum in ethical practice (see Homan, 1991). One of the problems with using codes of ethical practice as anything other than a baseline is that they can have the effect of forestalling rather than initiating the researcher's active and continuing engagement with the issues. I think it is important, therefore, to ask the following questions in relation to the criteria you think you are using to make your ethical decisions, and the complex range of interests you have identified in relation to your research:

Whose interests are served by these criteria?

How and why were they developed (either formally or informally)?

Do the different sources offer criteria of equal stringency?

Are they good enough in relation to the complex interests I have identified?

The morality, ethics and politics of research are at the same time complicated and important, and we shall return to them at many points in subsequent chapters.

PUTTING IT ALL TOGETHER: PRODUCING A RESEARCH DESIGN

So far I have encouraged the reader to pay a great deal of attention to intellectual and ethical issues in producing a research design, but I have said little about practical matters. This is not because I think practicalities are unimportant – far from it – but because it is essential that one's research design is not guided entirely by them. Instead, I think it is better to adopt the rule of dealing with practical issues in ways which are intellectually sound, even if practical considerations mean that you cannot do what you would ideally like to do in intellectual terms. The alternative is that you risk becoming overwhelmed by practical concerns and neglect some of the important intellectual ones dealt with above.

You will need to plan carefully what can be achieved given your resources, for example, time, money, equipment, transport, available data sources, your own abilities, skills and need for training, the likelihood of gaining access to key data sources. It is important to be realistic rather than optimistic in your plans, because resources have a tendency to go less far than you anticipate. You may be required to produce costings or a budget for your project and, whether or not you are compelled to do this, it can be a good way of focusing your mind on what really will be involved. It is important to remember that your own time is neither economically free, nor freely available.

It is with these kinds of practicalities in mind that you should begin to reassess your research questions and your research design, considering:

> What is possible given my resources?

> What is the most sensible use of my resources in relation to my research questions?

For example, if your resources will allow you to answer only one of your questions, or answer several but partially, which is the best strategy in terms of the intellectual puzzle you have identified? Whatever else, you will need to modify your research questions, and select from them, bearing in mind both the intellectual issues, and the practical ones. And it is this blend of intellectual and practical concerns which your research design should encapsulate. The most useful form of research design for you the researcher is one which is essentially a plan of what you are going to do. You can set this out in a variety of ways, and I do not think that there is any one rigid format which you should follow. Nevertheless, your research design should begin with your research questions and your intellectual puzzle, and then spell out how you intend to research these. It should make clear what overall methodological and analytical strategy you intend to adopt, what data sources and data generation methods you intend to use, what sampling and selection strategies you will use, what volume of work you intend to do (for example, how many interviews, documents, cases), how long each part of the process is likely to take, what other resources it will consume and, most importantly, why you are doing it in the way you have planned. In my view, you need to have worked your way through all of the questions set out in this chapter (and indeed many of those in subsequent chapters) in order to be able to achieve this kind of research design, whether or not your design actually explicitly incorporates all the answers to them.

Having said this, I should also emphasize that qualitative research designs invariably need to allow for flexibility, and for decision making to take place as the research process proceeds. Especially if you are working with an ontological and epistemological model where theory is generated from empirical data, and data generation and sampling decisions are made in the light of the evolving theoretical analysis, then you cannot – and will not want to – specify in advance all the details of your research design, numbers and types of cases you will draw on, and so on. In these circumstances it is useful to indicate in your initial research design that there will be points or times when further research decisions will need to be made, and to anticipate that you will produce several research designs sequentially, as your research strategy and practice evolves – each one giving you the opportunity to ask yourself similar sets of difficult questions, and to reflect on what you have achieved so far. These may of course be linked to a pilot study conducted early on in your research, whose purpose may be to try out sampling strategies, data generation and analytical techniques, to firm up on your intellectual puzzle and your research questions, or to allow you to gain experience of some aspects of the research process. However, postponing certain decisions until such a point as you have the necessary materials or conditions to deal with them is emphatically not the same as failing to design and plan your research. The big questions about research strategy, and the logic and principles of your methodology, really do need to be addressed right from the beginning, so that you are equipped to make further strategic decisions when the right time comes.

CONCLUSION

In this chapter I have attempted to guide the reader into the kind of thinking and self-interrogation which I believe is needed in order to be able to produce a good qualitative research design. I have not set out a standard format for a qualitative research design, partly because I do not think such a thing exists, but also because I see research design as a skilled activity requiring critical and creative thinking, rather than as a product which can be displayed and copied. In a sense, to display a standard product is likely to reduce rather than enhance the potential for creative thinking.

I have emphasized throughout the value of engaging oneself with difficult questions, and should add that it is crucial to keep a good account of your answers to these, and the reasoning process through which you arrive at your answers. This can become part of a research diary, or notes which you record on particular topics and issues, but whatever form it takes needs to be accessible to you both now and later, when you may wish to reconstruct, justify and defend the logic of your own personal research strategy. At many points in this chapter I have referred the reader to subsequent discussions in the book. This is because you will need to have thought your way though the whole research process in order to be able to make useful planning decisions.

There is perhaps little in this chapter which is distinctively about qualitative research. The flexibility and sequential nature of research designs is more characteristic of projects which are primarily qualitative in nature, but most of the other issues and questions in my view should apply to any research design in the social sciences, and of course many do incorporate both qualitative and quantitative approaches.

NOTE

1 This research project was entitled 'Inheritance, Property and Family Relationships'. It was funded by the Economic and Social Research Council (grant no. R00232035) and directed by Prof. Janet Finch, Dr Jennifer Mason, and Prof. Judith Masson. It was carried out at Lancaster University between 1990 and 1993.

FURTHER READING

Blaikie, N. (1993) *Approaches to Social Enquiry*, Cambridge: Polity (especially Chapters 4 and 7)
Brewer, J. and Hunter, A. (1989) *Multimethod Research: a Synthesis of Styles*. London: Sage
Fielding, N.G. and Fielding, J.L. (1986) *Linking Data*, London: Sage
Homan, R. (1991) *The Ethics of Social Research*, London: Longman
Hughes, J. (1990) *The Philosophy of Social Research*, 2nd edn, London: Longman
Marshall, C. and Rossman, G.B. (1995) *Designing Qualitative Research*, 2nd edn, London: Sage
Maykut, P. and Morehouse, R. (1994) *Beginning Qualitative Research: a Philosophical and Practical Guide*, London: Falmer (especially Chapter 2)
Rose, H. (1994) *Love, Power and Knowledge: towards a Feminist Transformation of the Sciences*, Cambridge: Polity
Smith, D. (1988) *The Everyday World as Problematic: a Feminist Sociology,* Milton Keynes: Open University Press
Stanley, L. and Wise, S. (1993) *Breaking Out Again: Feminist Ontology and Epistemology*, London: Routledge
Yin, R.K. (1989) *Case Study Research: Design and Methods*, London: Sage (especially Chapters 1 and 2)

3

GENERATING QUALITATIVE DATA: INTERVIEWING

In the last chapter we explored the question of research design. We touched on some of the key elements in the research process, because researchers need to take these into account when planning and designing their projects. This chapter begins our more detailed analysis of those elements of the research process, and of the difficult questions which researchers need to confront throughout it, by focusing on methods used for generating qualitative data. The chapter begins with a general discussion of issues connected with data, data sources, and data generation. I use the term *generating* rather than, for example, *collecting* data, for good reasons which I shall discuss below. The chapter goes on to consider in some detail the first of four broad approaches to method which are discussed in this book: qualitative interviewing. This approach to method is considered first, and in some detail, for three reasons. First, most qualitative researchers at some stage use some form of qualitative interviewing. Many use this as their main method for generating data. Secondly, many of the principles and issues raised in a discussion of qualitative interviewing are relevant to other methods also. And thirdly, qualitative interviewing actually can involve some techniques more commonly associated with other methods, for example, observing, generating and using documents. The following chapter uses the general framework established in this chapter to discuss three other broad approaches to method: observation, generating and using documents, and generating and using visual data.

DATA, SOURCES AND METHODS

It is important to begin with a few words about data sources. I want to begin by making a distinction between data sources on the one hand, and methods for generating data from those sources on the other, although I am going to suggest that this is a distinction which ultimately is likely to become blurred. An example will help to illustrate why such a distinction is nevertheless useful at the outset. You may, for example, see 'people' as data sources in the sense that they are repositories of knowledge, evidence, experience or whatever, which is relevant to your research. However, there may be a much wider range of methods through which you might contemplate generating data from people: for example, you might observe them, you might talk to them, you might collect products they had generated such as diaries, photographs and so on. In this sense, your data sources are those places or phenomena from or through which you believe data can be generated (ask yourself, potentially, could I generate data from this source?); your data generation methods are the techniques and strategies which you use to do this. If you start thinking in terms of this distinction between data sources and methods it does not mean that you are seeing data 'out there' as an already existing stock of knowledge, ready to be collected and independent of our interpretations as researchers. Many qualitative researchers would, of course, balk at that view, and my use of the term data 'generation' rather than a term like data 'collection' is intended to encapsulate the much wider range of relationships between researcher, social world, and data which qualitative research spans. I think it is more accurate to speak of *generating* data than *collecting* data, precisely because most qualitative perspectives would reject the idea that a researcher can be a completely neutral collector of information about the social world. Instead the researcher is seen as actively constructing knowledge about that world according to certain principles and using certain methods derived from their epistemological position. Therefore, as a researcher you do not simply work out where to find data which already exist in a collectable state. Instead you work out how best you can generate data from your chosen data sources. For this reason, the term *method* in qualitative research generally is meant to imply more than a practical technique or procedure for gaining data. It implies also a data generation process involving activities which are intellectual, analytical and interpretive.

You may find, therefore, that the distinction between data source and method of data generation begins to blur as your thinking and your research progress, but it is a useful starting point because it will help you to stretch your mind as widely as possible in your search for knowledge and evidence relevant to your research questions. To begin with, then, I want to reflect upon the wide range of possible data sources available to qualitative researchers. In the previous chapter I suggested that, initially at least, it is a good idea to allow yourself to think widely and creatively about possible data sources and methods, even though you will sharpen and focus these initial thoughts in the light of the intellectual and practical considerations of your research design. So you will wish to ask yourself:

What data sources might I use?

Here are some possible answers. They are not mutually exclusive.

- people (or you might be more specific about what it is about people which you think represents a data source, for example, people's

experiences, accounts, interpretations, memories, opinions, understandings, thoughts, ideas, emotions, feelings, perceptions, morals,
behaviours, practices, actions, activities, conversations, interactions,
humour, faith, creations, products, secrets, relationships)
- speech
- language
- writing
- texts
- narratives, stories
- art, cultural products
- visual images, diagrams, photographs, maps
- publications
- media products
- documents, archives
- laws, statutes, rules, regulations
- policies
- collectivities, groups, clubs
- organizations
- events
- socio-geographical locations.

These are simply a few examples of phenomena which qualitative researchers may see as data sources. Some researchers would see all items in
this list as being essentially to do with 'people' as a data source. Others
would see many of the items as data sources in their own right. Whatever
answers you choose, they will need to tie in with your ontological view of
social reality, and your epistemological view of how that reality can be
known. So you will need to ask:

> How well does the use of these data
> sources match my ontological
> perspective on what constitutes the
> social world, and my epistemological
> perspective on how knowledge
> about that world can be produced?

In thinking about the available data sources for your own research, you will
also need to consider:

> What are the practicalities of using
> these data sources?

Do they actually exist, or can they be generated? For example, are there people with the appropriate range of experiences? Have relevant photographs or texts been produced in a form which is appropriate (or can they be produced)?

What are the ethics of using these data sources?

For example, is it consistent with your ethical position to access private diaries or letters, or to search out people with the experiences in which you are interested? Are there ethical difficulties in using these sources, irrespective of the methods of data generation you might choose?

In thinking through your answers to these questions, you will of course be beginning to engage with the question of method, that is, *how* you can generate data from your sources. You may find that it is possible to think of a wide range of methods for generating data from your data sources, or you may feel that there is very little choice. As I have stated, in this chapter and the next we are going to discuss four methods: interviews, observation, the generation and use of documents, and the generation and use of visual data. We will see that these broad headings actually can in practice encompass a wide variety of methods and techniques, and also that what you see as a legitimate and appropriate method will depend, in large part, on what your perspective is prepared to count as data and as evidence.

QUALITATIVE INTERVIEWING: LOGIC AND RATIONALE

The term 'qualitative interviewing' is usually intended to refer to in-depth, semi-structured or loosely structured forms of interviewing. Burgess calls them 'conversations with a purpose' (1984: 102). Generally, these types of interviews are characterized by:

- a relatively informal style, for example with the appearance of a conversation or discussion rather than a formal question and answer format

- a thematic, topic-centred, biographical or narrative approach, for example where the researcher does not have a structured list of questions, but does usually have a range of topics, themes or issues which s/he wishes to cover

- the assumption that data are generated via the interaction, because either the interviewee(s), or the interaction itself, are the data sources.

Qualitative interviews may involve one to one interactions, or larger groups.

You may notice that what passes for a qualitative interview varies amongst the different social science disciplines, and to some extent within them. Thus, for some researchers, a qualitative interview is always and necessarily semi-structured or loosely structured, whereas for others a qualitative interview can be based on open ended questions in an otherwise structured interview schedule. My discussion is based on a definition which is rather more like the first example than the second.

Interviews are one of the most commonly recognized forms of qualitative research method. Perhaps for this reason, it is not uncommon for a researcher to *assume* that their study will involve some such interviews, without spending time working out why it should, why they want to use qualitative interviews, and what they expect to get out of them. In my discussion of research design in Chapter 2 I suggested that you should ask yourself these questions about any of the methods you are considering using. For qualitative interviewing, the questions you should ask of yourself might look like this:

> Why might I want to use *interviews*?
> Why might I want to speak to or
> interact with people to generate data?

> Why might I want to use *qualitative*
> interviewing? Why this style and
> approach rather than a more
> structured form of interviewing or
> questionnaire?

Your answers to these questions are likely to be quite complex and of course need to be closely related to your research questions (see Chapter 2). Here are some possible reasons why you might wish to use qualitative interviewing as a method.

- Your *ontological* position suggests that people's knowledge, views, understandings, interpretations, experiences, and interactions are meaningful properties of the social reality which your research questions are designed to explore.

- Your *epistemological* position suggests that a legitimate way to generate data on these ontological properties is to interact with people, to talk to them, to listen to them, and to gain access to their accounts and articulations. You should, however, be aware of epistemological shortcomings of interviewing in this respect too. For example, if you are interested in people's experiences, these can only be *recounted* in interviews. If you are interested in people's interpretations and under-standings you must bear in mind that talking to people will not enable you to get inside their heads, and that you will only be able to gain access to those interpretations and understandings which are revealed in some way in an interview.

There are other epistemological reasons for conducting interviews however. You may for example feel that knowledge and evidence are contextual, situational and interactional, and that this requires you to take a distinctive approach to getting at what you really want to know about in each interview. If this is the case your interviews may need to be flexible and sensitive to the specific dynamics of each interaction, so that you are, effectively, tailor-making each one on the spot. Furthermore, what you want to know about may be rather complex, or may not be clearly formulated in your interviewees' minds in a way which they can simply articulate in response to a short standardized question. You may be interested in the ways in which people work out and articulate their understandings and responses, or the ways in which they interact with you (and you with them). You may want to take cues from your interviewees about what to ask them, rather than to go into the interaction pre-scripted, so that you can follow up their specific responses along lines which are peculiarly relevant to them and their context, and which you could not have anticipated in advance. You may wish to follow the narrative or sequence provided by the interviewee.

Whichever of these apply, you are likely to be making certain kinds of epistemological assumptions about the *interaction* between yourself as researcher and those you are researching, which suggest that semi-structured interviewing is appropriate. These assumptions will be very different to those which form the basis for structured interviews or questionnaires, which are very often designed to minimize 'bias' through the standardization of the questions which are asked, and sometimes through the standardization of the way they are asked, and of the interviewers asking them. The underlying assumption here is that bias can be eradicated or controlled, and that – in stimulus–response fashion – if you standardize the stimulus, then any variations seen in responses will be a true measure, rather than an artefact of your methods. You, on the other hand, may feel that interviews are always social interactions, however structured or unstructured the researcher tries to make them, and that it is inappropriate to see social interaction as 'bias' which can potentially be eradicated. From this point of view you cannot separate the interview from the social interaction in which it was produced, and you should not try. It is better to try to understand the complexities of the interaction, rather than to pretend that key dimensions can be controlled for. At the very least, you will probably reject the idea that standardization of questions and format ensures that interviewees will hear and interpret the questions in standardized ways, or that their standardized articulations genuinely express standardized meanings. If this is your approach, you need nevertheless to ask yourself to what extent it is ever possible fully to understand the complexities of the interview interaction.

- Your view of the ways in which *social explanations* can be constructed lays emphasis on depth, complexity and roundedness in data, rather than the kind of broad surveys of surface patterns which, for example, questionnaires might provide. So, for example, you may wish to explain something about social process, social change, social organization, social meaning, and you will argue that this requires an understanding of depth and complexity in, say, people's accounts and experiences, rather than a more superficial analysis of surface comparability between accounts of large numbers of people. In other words, you may wish to achieve depth and roundedness of understanding in these areas, rather than a broad understanding of surface patterns. This is likely to mean that you take a distinctive approach to comparison, to analysing data and to the construction of explanations. So, for example, you are unlikely to rely heavily on quantifying, although you may want to count or enumerate certain elements of your data. At the very least, your approach to making analytical comparisons in your data set will not depend upon having asked all interviewees the same set of questions. You will assume that in order to achieve data which are comparable in key ways, far from giving everyone standardized questions in a standardized form, you may well need to ask different questions of your different interviewees. Your point of comparison is therefore unlikely to be straightforwardly sited at the level of differences or similarities in people's answers to the same set of questions. What and where your points of comparison are must depend upon your research questions, and the analytical principles you propose to use or develop, but they are likely to be conceptual rather than straightforwardly empirical, and 'inductively' generated through your data (see Chapter 7 for a further discussion). You are likely to want to identify interpretive themes in your data upon which to construct your analysis and your argument. Nevertheless, you will need to engage with the question of how you ensure that you are generating data which will allow appropriate comparisons to be made.

- You wish to conceptualize *yourself as active and reflexive* in the process of data generation, rather than as a neutral data collector, and you are going to analyse your role within this process. Whilst most qualitative researchers do have this kind of aspiration, it is important not to underestimate the reflexive challenge posed by analysing your own role within the research process.

- Rather more pragmatically, *the data you want may not feasibly be available in any other form*, so that asking people for their accounts, talking and listening to them and so on, is the only way to get at what you are interested in. For example, records of existing research, documents, letters, diaries, and so on, which you might use if you could, may not exist, or perhaps direct observation of phenomena in which you are interested is simply impossible. If this is your reason for using qualitative interviews, then you need to consider how good a substitute for your preferred method is a 'conversation with a purpose' of this kind. Does it really get at what you are interested in? Is it accurate and reliable?

- You may indeed wish to use qualitative interviewing as just *one of several methods* to explore your research questions. Qualitative interviews may add an additional dimension, or may help you to approach your questions from a different angle, or in greater depth, and so on (see Chapters 2 and 4 for a discussion of integrating different methods). You may be attempting some form of methodological triangulation, where you are using interviewing in tandem with another method to see how well they corroborate each other. For example, you may interview selected participants from a meeting for which you have a set of minutes, so that you can make comparisons between the different types of account of the same event and set of interactions. As I suggested in Chapter 2, however, you need to think carefully about how far different methods can actually corroborate each other. Do they actually yield data on similar or the same phenomena? Do they yield comparable data?

- You may have a particular view of *research ethics and politics* which means that you believe interviewees should be given more freedom in and control of the interview situation than is permitted with 'structured' approaches. You may want to suggest that qualitative interviewing is more likely to generate a fairer and fuller representation of the interviewees' perspectives. You may believe that you, as interviewer, should be more responsive in the interview interaction than a structured format allows, for example answering questions the interviewee may ask, giving information, opinions, support. Or you may feel it is important to try to make sure your interviewees enjoy being interviewed, and your view may be that qualitative interviewing is the best way to achieve that. Nevertheless, you should ask yourself to what extent qualitative interviewing achieves your ethical goals. For example, does it give interviewees more control, does it inevitably represent their perspectives more fully and fairly, is it enjoyable?

PLANNING AND CONDUCTING QUALITATIVE INTERVIEWS

Good qualitative interviewing is hard, creative, work. It is a much more complex and exhausting task to plan and carry out a qualitative interview than, for example, to develop and use a structured questionnaire for asking a set of predetermined questions. In that sense the informal and conversational style of this form of interviewing belies a much more rigorous set of activities.

To begin with, qualitative interviews require a great deal of planning. For the moment I am leaving aside the question of deciding who you want to interview and gaining access to them, since this is dealt with in the discussion of sampling and selection in Chapter 5. What I mean by planning, therefore, is all the other work which goes into preparing for your interviews. Just because you are planning a loosely structured or semi-structured interview which is going to feel (to the interviewee) like a 'conversation with a purpose', this does not mean that you do not need to engage in some detailed and rigorous planning. In fact, in my view qualitative interviewers have to work particularly hard on the structure and flow of the interview. However, given that most qualitative researchers will find the idea of preparing this in advance in the form of a structured sequence of questions unsatisfactory (for the reasons outlined above), they must use alternative mechanisms and they must develop a rather specific set of intellectual and social skills. I do not think the importance of these, and the challenge of acquiring them, can be overestimated.

First, we shall consider what it is that qualitative interviewers have to prepare for: what kinds of challenges are they likely to face in the interview situation? Then we shall discuss how that preparation might be done. Basically, in the absence of a predesigned set and sequence of questions, the qualitative interviewer has to prepare themselves to be able to 'think on their feet' in the interview itself. They have to do this quickly, effectively, coherently and in ways which are consistent with their research questions. They need to be able to ensure that the interview interaction actually does generate relevant data, which means simultaneously orchestrating the intellectual and social dynamics of the situation. It is all too easy to orchestrate a pleasant social encounter whose content has little or no bearing on the intellectual puzzle which the research is designed to address. A qualitative interviewer has to be ready to make on the spot decisions about the content and sequence of the interview as it progresses. You will find you are asking yourself the following questions about *substance* and *style*, *scope* and *sequence* – and, if you are well prepared, you will have thought about how to handle these in advance. We shall discuss how you might prepare yourself shortly.

> How should I ask my questions?
> What *substance*? What *style*?

Working out how to ask questions means both how to phrase them, or what words to use, and also what kind of manner, demeanour and approach you are going to adopt. You will not have a standard script of questions, and will instead need to think on the spot how best to ask about whatever it is that you 'really want to know'. This means that you will need to be able to formulate appropriate questions there and then, rather than asking your interviewee to wait while you fumble in your notes for a preformulated question which you discover, as you ask it, is not suitable in this particular case. This process involves more than thinking of the right words. Whilst I do not wish to suggest that we all could or should simply select appropriate demeanours and approaches 'off the peg' and slip them on and off at will, I do want to emphasize that you will find yourself making decisions about how best to go about asking questions and how best to conduct and present yourself in the interview through the questions you are asking and the way you are asking them. Your decisions will be likely to depend upon your research questions and your intellectual puzzle, the specific situational dynamics of each interview, and what repertoire of demeanours you personally are able to draw upon.

> How much depth or breadth do I want to achieve on these issues? What should be the *scope* of my questions?

Just as working out what to ask, and in what sequence to ask it, depends upon on the spot assessments of the relevance of each part of the interview interaction to your intellectual puzzle and research questions, so too does deciding upon how deeply you want to engage with any one particular issue, or how broadly you want to cover a range of issues. You may find yourself having to make decisions about the implications of sacrificing some breadth of coverage for depth on a particular issue in a particular case. You may find you are having difficulty achieving either breadth or depth, because your interviewee(s) is or are garrulous in ways which are not entirely relevant, so you may have to make an on the spot decision about how to get the best – in terms of breadth or depth – out of that particular interaction.

> What should I ask next? What should be the *sequence*?

Probably the easiest part is deciding where to begin the interview, and you may well wish to begin all your interviews with a similar opening or 'warm up' question or topic. But as each interview progresses you need constantly to make decisions about what to ask next in the context of that particular interview. This means working out whether you want to ask a question which relates to what you and your interviewee(s) have just been talking about, or whether you want to change the subject and move the interview onto new terrain. Whichever of these you decide to do, the social task is to orchestrate an interaction which moves easily and painlessly between topics and questions. The intellectual task is to try to assess, on the spot, the relevance of each part of the interaction to your research questions, or to 'what you really want to know'. Although you are likely to have some form of *aide-mémoire* to remind you about the topics and issues you are interested in, you nevertheless need to be able to make connections between relevant issues quickly, and to spot and follow up issues which may be relevant, but which you had not anticipated.

These three questions all imply the need to make quick, but considered and strategic, decisions while you are interviewing. In each case, these decisions and their consequences will need to:

- make sense to, or be meaningful to, the interviewee(s)
- be related to your interviewee's(s') circumstances, experiences and so on, based on what you already know about them
- be sensitive to the interviewee(s), to their needs and rights, in accordance with your ethical position
- help the flow of the interview interaction – the 'conversation with a purpose' – rather than impede it
- ensure an appropriate focus on issues and topics relevant to your research questions.

Clearly, taken together these represent a formidable task for which a high degree of intellectual and social skill is required. At any one time you may be: listening to what the interviewee(s) is or are currently saying and trying to interpret what they mean; trying to work out whether what they are saying has any bearing on 'what you really want to know'; trying to think in new and creative ways about 'what you really want to know'; trying to pick up on any changes in your interviewees' demeanour and interpret these, for example you may notice they are becoming reticent for reasons which you do not understand, or if there is more than one interviewee there may be some tension developing between them; reflecting on something they said 20 minutes ago; formulating an appropriate response to what they are currently saying; formulating the next question which might involve shifting the interview onto new terrain; keeping an eye on your watch and making decisions about depth and breadth given your time limits. At the same time you will be observing what is going on around the interview; you may be making notes or, if you are audio or video tape recording the interview, keeping half an eye on your equipment to ensure that it is working; and you may be dealing with 'distractions' like a wasp which you think is about to sting you, a pet dog which is scratching itself loudly directly in front of your tape recorder microphone, a telephone which keeps ringing, a child crying, and so on.

How might qualitative interviewers prepare for such a challenging set of tasks? First, it is vital that researchers work on developing the skills they need to handle the social, intellectual and indeed practical elements of these kinds of interactions, and on preparing for their interviews, rather than assuming that these are attributes which they either do or do not have already. It is possible, for example, to practise the following:

- listening – *really* listening – to what people are saying. Most people need a great deal of practice in this. You need to be able to do this whether or not you are tape recording your interviews.

- remembering what people have said to you, and indeed what you have already asked them. It is only too easy, in the context of the multiple activities you are engaging in, to forget what you have been told, or what you yourself have already said. If you are conducting more than one interview per day, you may become unclear about what occurred in one and what in another.

- achieving a good balance between talking and listening. The appropriate balance is likely to vary in different situations, and there is no general rule about what you should do. However, it is important to be aware of what you are doing, and of the implications of it. So, for example, are you interrupting your interviewees frequently? For what reasons? What are you trying to achieve by interrupting? Do you achieve it? Is interrupting in this way helpful, or unhelpful?

- observing, picking up verbal and non-verbal cues about the social situation, and the mood of your interviewee(s). This means making sure you are tuned in to body language and to demeanour so that you are recognizing when people become bored, tired, angry, upset, embarrassed. Sometimes, you may recognize a change in your interviewee(s)' demeanour, but be unable to interpret it.

- becoming accomplished in the practicalities of interviewing, for example, in note-taking, in using your tape recorder (see section below on generating data for a discussion of some of these aspects).

All of these skills involve handling the social interaction of the interview appropriately. You can practise them in everyday social situations, or with your peers, colleagues, or advisers, or better still in a pilot study which you can reflect upon later. You can audio or video tape record some pilot interviews, and scrutinize the recording later on for these aspects as well as taking the opportunity to train yourself in the use of the equipment. Or you can ask a colleague to sit in on some pilot interviews and give you their views about how you are handling the situation. Or you might want to ask your pilot interviewees what they think. In general, you need to find some mechanism for ensuring that you are identifying which skills you need to work on, and that you are developing and improving these.

Whilst preparing for the social interaction of qualitative interviews is very important, there is also a great deal of intellectual preparation. As I have pointed out, you are highly unlikely to find yourself producing a structured list of questions which you can simply reel off in the interview. Instead, you need to develop a mechanism to help you to devise the intellectual skills you will need to make on the spot decisions about the substance and style, scope and sequence of questions outlined above, for whilst the decisions have to be made and acted upon quickly, they should nevertheless be strategic and considered rather than *ad hoc* and idiosyncratic. I have emphasized the need to ground your decisions in your intellectual puzzle and your research questions. Although this does not mean that you should produce a rigid interview structure in advance, or that you must try to anticipate everything in which you are likely to be interested, it does mean that you need to be clear enough about recognizing what you might be interested in to be able to judge what to pursue in the interviews. There may be qualitative researchers who will disagree with me here, because they wish to emphasize the possibilities for exploratory and *un*structured data *collection*. However, as I argued in Chapter 2, my view is that, whether or not they acknowledge it, all researchers *do* have ontological and epistemological positions which get activated or expressed in their research decisions and judgements, and I now want to add that all researchers do make decisions and judgements in the conduct of their qualitative interviews. Therefore, I do not think it is possible to 'collect' data in a wholly unstructured way through a qualitative interview, because the decisions and judgements the researcher makes give some form of structure and purpose to the data generation process.

Given this, my concern is with the kinds of procedures which qualitative researchers can use to help them make sensible, intellectually compelling and systematic interpretations and judgements. Whatever technical system you develop and use to do this, you will need to make sure that it is one which has the effect of firmly entrenching your research questions and your intellectual puzzle in your head, because it will usually be on the basis of fast mental reasoning, rather than slow reference to notes and reminders, that you will make important decisions. Although you are likely to take written or visual notes and aids into your interviews to supplement your thinking, you will inevitably want to make many decisions and judgements quickly, without always referring to your notes.

Figure 3.1 gives an example of a procedure which you might use to prepare and plan intellectually for qualitative interviews. It is intended not to be rigid or prescriptive, but instead to give a sense of the kind of work which needs to be done in advance of interviews, and suggestions about how that might be achieved. It uses a worked example based on a real piece of research which I introduced in Chapter 2, entitled 'Inheritance, Property and Family Relationships'. Figure 3.2 provides a simplified overview of the same procedure.

Figure 3.1   *Example of planning and preparation for qualitative interviewing*

Step 1

List or assemble the 'big' research questions which the study is designed to explore.

Example of one of the 'big' research questions in the 'Inheritance' project
  1   *How do families handle issues of inheritance?*

Step 2

Break down or subdivide the big research questions into 'mini' research questions. The links between the big questions and the subcategories of them – the mini questions – should be clearly expressed, for example by using corresponding numbers or codes, or by laying the two sets of questions out in a chart, or by using cross-referenced index cards. It is possible to establish a perfectly workable manual system, or you can use a computer graphics package and/or database to help you.

Example of mini research questions which are subcategories of the big research question given above
  1   (a) *Are negotiations about inheritance treated as part of a wider set of negotiations about support in families? Or is inheritance treated as a totally separate matter?*
       (b) *Do people in any way take into account the possibility of inheritance in formulating their own life plans?*
       (c) *Is a clear distinction maintained between 'blood relatives' and 'in-laws' in the process of negotiating inheritance?*

Step 3

For each mini research question, start to develop ideas about how it might be possible to get at the relevant issues in an interview situation. This means converting your big and mini examples of 'what you really want to know' into possible interview topics, and thinking of some possible questions – in terms of their substance, and the style you might use to ask them. These will not form a rigid 'script' for you to use in the interview, but the process of developing possible topics and questions will get you thinking in ways appropriate to an interview interaction. Again, make sure that the links between this set of questions and the other two (that is the big and mini research questions) are clearly expressed.

Examples of interview topics and questions related to mini research questions
  1   (a) *Family inheritance history, and history of other family support – what happened in practice in relation to specific events and instances? How did people decide what was the most appropriate course of action?*

(b) *Knowledge of the inheritance plans, content of wills etc., of other family members. Have people thought about inheritance at all? Have they made wills? Do people have life plans, for example, do people have a sense of what they will be doing, where living, and so on, in 5 or 10 or 20 years' time? How were these plans arrived at?*

(c) *Ascertain composition of family and kin group, and what kinds of relationships exist with specific others. Explore whom people count as 'blood kin', whom as 'in-laws' or 'step-relatives' — establish this so that family inheritance history, and specific events and instances, can be contextualized in the sense that we will know the 'kin status' (as conceptualized by the interviewee) of relevant parties. Explore the detail of distributions of assets, and negotiations about them, in relation to kin of different status. Who has legitimate interests? How do people decide whom to include and exclude? Possibly ask directly whether people think about their blood relatives and their in-laws in different ways in relation to inheritance, and other matters.*

Step 4

Cross-reference all the levels, if you have not done so already, so that you know that each big research question has a set of corresponding mini research questions, and each of these has a set of ideas about interview topics and questions. Make sure the cross-referencing works in reverse, so that your interview topics and questions really are going to help you to answer your big research questions.

Step 5

Start to develop some ideas about a loose structure, or format, for interviews. You will want this to be highly flexible and variable, but you should be able to produce some kind of guide to the key issues and types of questions you will want to discuss.

Example of loose interview structure/format developed for the 'Inheritance' project

In this project we developed a loose interview format, based on key topics and types of questions we were likely to want to ask. With each interviewee we anticipated following up lines of enquiry specific to their circumstances, which we would not be able to anticipate in advance. We therefore wanted maximum flexibility, but also some kind of guide or prompt for the interviewer about the key issues and questions with which the study was concerned. We did not produce a script of questions, but rather a set of index cards to take into each interview. One card contained a flow chart of a possible interview structure, which could be readily modified on the spot. The other cards contained shorthand notes about specific topics and issues for the inter- viewer's use at relevant points in the interview. These notes were non- sequential, so that they could be drawn upon at any time, in relation to the specific context of the interview in progress. Here are examples of each type of card:

'Loose structure/format of interview' card

Possible main structure	Specific topics and issues – to be asked in relation to any of the main structure sections (there are cards for each of these sets of questions)
Introductory explanation ↓	
Brief social/personal characteristics ↓	
Composition of kin group and spouse's kin group ↓	Inheritance history, other responsibilities and relationships, inheritance family and kin group
Family inheritance history ↓	
Specific questions (if not covered elsewhere) ↓	Formal and external factors, including the law
Questions about the law check ↓	Principles and processes of inheritance and family responsibility
Personal characteristics check	Social and personal characteristics (current and over time)

'Example of specific topics and issues' card
Inheritance history, other responsibilities and relationships, inheritance family and kin group

Experience of inheritance: personal/others – as testator, beneficiary, executor; patterns characteristic of own family; how many generations; experience of legal procedures and services; expected and unexpected; experience of will making; when, why; professional advice; intestacy laws; lifetime transfers.

Inheritance and other aspects of kin relationships/wider patterns of responsibility: family relationships affected by inheritance? conscious of possible inheritance in relationships with relatives?; conflicts – how resolved; life plans and inheritance e.g. housing, geography, timing; death and how it is dealt with; making formal statements about relationships?; part of ongoing reciprocity and exchange – explicit/implicit?; idea of final settlement?

The inheritance family or kin group: who has legitimate interests?; in-laws/step-relatives/secondary kin?; exclusions and principles of exclusion/inclusion; inheriting via someone else.

Step 6

Work out whether you want to include *any* standardized questions or sections in your interviews. There may be certain questions which you want to ensure that you ask everybody. In the example above the introductory explanation was fairly standardized, as were some of the questions about personal and social characteristics (for example, age, marital status). You might also want to think of some standardized comments and assurances which you will make about confidentiality of data to your interviewees.

Step 7

Cross-check that your format, and any standardized questions or sections, do cover adequately and appropriately your possible topics and questions.

TURNING QUALITATIVE INTERVIEWS INTO DATA

So far we have focused on the planning and doing of qualitative interviews, but have said little about processes through which what we call data are produced. I am referring here to the mechanisms through which you transform your interview interaction into what you consider to be data. This throws the spotlight back onto epistemological issues and, in particular, onto what your perspective suggests count as data and as evidence. You will need to consider the following types of questions:

> What procedures give my interview interactions the status of data? Do different procedures yield data of differing status or quality?

In answering these questions you need to ask yourself what it is that turns your interviews into data, rather than just chats or conversations. Do the procedures, or the data, have to be verifiable in some way in order to have the status of good or reliable data? What principles of verification might be appropriate? This raises further questions as follows.

> Does my own written or tape recorded account, and do my written or tape recorded fieldnotes, which are based on my interpretations of what went on, count as data?

Figure 3.2   *Overview of the planning and preparation procedure for qualitative interviews*

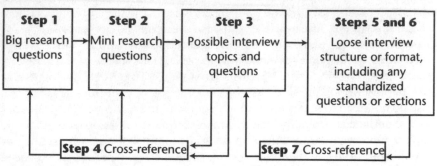

In particular, how can you be sure that you are not simply inventing data, or getting it 'wrong'? It is very important in this context to record as fully and explicitly as you can the route by which you came to the interpretations you are making. This will involve questioning your own assumptions. You need to remember that, however 'objective' you try to be in your records, you are continually making judgements about what to write down or record, what you have observed, heard and experienced, what you think it means. Your records need to provide the fullest possible justification for your own decisions. You should also remember, however, that this is one of the only ways in which you can produce, as data, an account of how you experienced the interview, of what judgements you were making throughout it, and so on.

Do my own memories and unwritten interpretations of the interview interaction count as data?

In answering this question you will inevitably face the issue of verifiability. How can you be sure that your memories are accurate? However, it would be naive to suggest that researchers do not use their memories and unwritten interpretations from time to time in their analyses. You need to try to be as systematic as you can about it.

Does the interview or interaction become data only when it becomes text as, for example, in a transcription of a tape recorded interview?

If you think the answer to this is yes, then do not forget that a transcription is always partial partly because it is an inadequate record of non-verbal aspects of the interaction (even if you try to insert these in the form of fieldnotes into the transcription afterwards), and also because judgements are made (usually by the person doing the transcription) about which verbal utterances to turn into text, and how to do it. For some verbal utterances, there simply are not written English translations! Therefore, do not assume that a transcription provides an 'objective record' of your interviews, or that you do not need to make a record of your own observations, interpretations and experiences of the interview. Make sure that the knowledge that you have a tape recorder switched on does not tempt you to stop listening or watching or doing all the other work outlined above. Not only do you need to continue with these activities in order to conduct the interview well, but you may discover subsequently that your equipment had failed. If you were not paying full attention to the interaction, there will be little you can retrieve from it.

> Would a visual or audio record of the interview count as data in itself?

If you think the answer is yes, then some of the same provisos apply as with transcriptions. Ask yourself which aspects of the interaction you do not gain access to via a video tape. For example, you will not have a record of what went on behind the camera. You may have a record from only one visual perspective. And, as with tape recording and transcribing, this does not give you much access to the interviewer's observations, interpretations, experiences and judgements.

> Is the verbal interchange of the interview alone data? Do other non-verbal aspects of the interaction and its context count?

Your answer to this is likely to be yes, and certainly so if you are doing a video recording. But if your answer is yes, then you need to think about how you ensure that you are generating data on these other aspects, and recording them systematically.

> Can diagrams, pictures, drawings,
> charts and photographs produced
> during the interview, or before or
> after it, count as data?

The production of these kinds of visual materials, or encouraging your interviewees to produce something of this kind, can be a very creative way of accessing aspects of your interviewees' lives or experiences which are non-verbalized, or difficult for them to verbalize. Do not assume, however, that everyone finds it easy to express themselves through the production of these kinds of materials. Nevertheless, these can be particularly useful if 'what you really want to know about' in ontological terms is not readily or appropriately expressed verbally. You can use visual materials as prompts in an interview, or you can produce charts or diagrams jointly with your interviewees, or you can ask them to produce their own 'cognitive maps' as drawings, diagrams (see Miles and Huberman, 1994, for lots of examples) or pictures. The latter technique is fairly widely used in interviews with children.

> Do I wish to derive data from
> interviews in a literal, interpretive or
> reflexive sense?

When thinking about all of these difficult questions, you may find it helpful to draw a distinction between literal, interpretive and reflexive 'readings' of interviews. If, for example, you wished to derive data in a *literal* sense, then you would probably be interested in aspects of the interaction such as the literal dialogue, including its form and sequence, or the literal substance. If you wished to derive data in an *interpretive* sense, then you would be wanting to 'read' the interviews for what you think they mean, or possibly for what you think you can infer about something outside of the interview interaction itself. And if you wished to derive data in a *reflexive* sense, then you would want to 'read' something about your role, and your interface with the interaction. The different decisions about what count as data which you can potentially make will imply different answers to these questions, and place differential emphasis on literal, interpretive or reflexive data. In practice, you may wish to derive data in all three ways, but it will nevertheless help you in doing so to think carefully about what kind of balance between them you are hoping to achieve.

In general, you should try to be as clear as you can about your answers to all of these questions as early as you can in your research process, since they will help you to choose your methods for generating (or recording) data from your interviews. You will need to think carefully about which methods are best for you – in both practical and intellectual terms. It is important to remember that tape recording or video recording, and transcribing in full, usually represent a very large commitment of time and resources. You should therefore be clear that you have good reasons for doing this, for example that you are interested in the ways in which people articulate their ideas, not just in the substance of what they say. These reasons should be closely linked to your research questions. You will also need to have some idea of how you are going to go about analysing your data, so that you make sure that what you generate takes an appropriate form for this type of analysis (see Chapters 6 and 7 for a further discussion of data analysis).

I think this demonstrates that it is possible to generate a fairly wide range of types of data from interviews, and that we should view interviews perhaps more creatively than the verbal to text-based data production devices they are sometimes thought to be. It also suggests that conducting interviews can help a researcher to develop experience in a fairly wide range of methods.

ETHICAL ISSUES IN QUALITATIVE INTERVIEWING

I emphasized the importance of ethical issues in research design in the previous chapter, and more generally the need to be clear about developing a set of ethical principles at each stage in the research process. I also suggested that this is by no means straightforward. The use of qualitative interviews as a data generation method raises a number of general ethical issues, and there will also be specific ethical concerns connected to any one particular project. Some of these can be anticipated in advance, but just as you will find yourself making intellectual and practical decisions on the spot, so too you will from time to time need to make hasty ethical judgements. You must prepare yourself to do this, by thinking through the kinds of ethical issues which might arise, and your possible responses to them. Whilst you cannot anticipate all of them, this will nevertheless help you to ensure that you are thinking and acting in an ethically principled way even in the face of the unexpected. Here are some examples of difficult questions about ethics and qualitative interviews which you can ask yourself as a form of preparation.

> How far is my own interview practice and style ethical?

> On what basis am I judging what is ethical and what is not?

> What justifications can I offer for the ethics of my interview practice and style?

> On what basis, and to whom, are these acceptable?

Answering these questions might involve thinking about:

- What you ask. Are you asking questions about personal or private matters, or matters which your interviewees do not wish to discuss? Are you asking about traumas, tragedies, mistakes, illegal activities? Are you asking questions which may distress, worry, or annoy your interviewees? In examples such as these, you will need to think about your ethical justifications.

- How you ask it. For example, are you using trick questions to catch your interviewees out, to confuse them? Are you doggedly pursuing a particular issue? Are you asking questions in a blunt way, to see how your interviewees react? Is your style of questioning making your interviewees uncomfortable?

- What you 'let' your interviewees tell you. Are your interviewees revealing more than you think they should? Even if you do not ask them directly, they may feel relaxed and open up to you about issues which you suspect they consider to be private. What are the ethical implications of the process of gaining your interviewees' trust, and the process of making your interview feel enjoyable, and like a conversation?

- Whether and how you can guarantee the confidentiality and anonymity of your interviewees, if this is what you have said you will do. You must think carefully about how you will fulfil such promises, and this can be quite difficult given the full, rich and personal nature of the data generated from qualitative interviews. Such data can usually be recognized by the interviewee whether or not you attach the interviewee's name to them, and also they may be recognizable to other people.

- The power relations of the interview interaction. It is usually assumed that the interviewer exercises power over the interviewee in and after the interview, for example in setting the agenda and in controlling the data. In this context you clearly have certain responsibilities to those interviewees. But power relations can be more complex and multidirectional than this, and sometimes they may simply be reversed – you may, for example, be interviewing very powerful people, and you may feel that they are controlling the agenda. You may feel your personal safety is at issue. In these cases, you must nevertheless think through the ethical implications, rather than assuming that ethics do not count because you as researcher are not wielding all the power.

> Have I gained the 'informed consent' of my interviewees for their participation?

Many of the ethical guidelines published by professional academic associations emphasize the importance of gaining the informed consent of all participants in research. On the face of it, this seems fairly straightforward where qualitative interviews are being used, since the participants are clearly identifiable, and can be asked whether or not they give their consent before the interview begins. However, I want to suggest that getting informed consent is actually quite a complex and difficult business even in this context. You will need to consider the following issues:

- Whose consent to ask. You should certainly gain the consent of the people you propose to interview. However, you should be careful about how readily you accept that consent has been gained. In particular, you should acknowledge the persuasive influences which operate on people when you ask them to consent to take part in your research, for example powerful committee members, teachers, parents, carers, employers, colleagues, yourself, all may influence a potential interviewee into saying yes. How much choice do interviewees really have about participating? Is it ever appropriate for a third party to give consent on someone else's behalf, for example a parent on behalf of a child, a relative or carer on behalf of someone with a mental illness, a husband on behalf of his wife, an employer on behalf of their employees? Is it ever desirable to gain the consent of someone other than the interviewee, for example a parent *as well as* the child you wish to interview? You need to recognize that it is not uncommon for an interviewee to reveal what seems like private information concerning third parties whose consent you have not gained.

- How to be sure that the consent you have gained is actually *informed* consent. This is very difficult, and relates crucially to what it is that you think you are asking people to give their consent to, and what rights you think they are giving to you in giving that consent. For example, are you asking them to consent to:

1   participating in the interview? Does this mean they are consenting to answer whatever questions you might ask? Are you giving them opportunities to withdraw their consent at any stage? You may wish to renegotiate consent at several points during the interaction, as the interviewee becomes more fully informed about what consenting to the interview actually means.

2   giving you the right to use the data generated through the interview in ways which you see fit? Do you think they understand and share your perspective on what counts as data, for example, where you are drawing on not only their words, but also their intonation, body language, pauses, general demeanour, what they say 'off the record' when the tape recorder is switched off, other aspects of the interaction?

3   giving you the right to interpret and analyse the data, making comparisons with data generated through other interactions? Most interviewees will be unfamiliar with the principles and techniques of analysis which you use, and with the ontological and epistemological principles upon which your research is based.

4   giving you the right to publish or reproduce the data, and the analysis?

In my view, there are limits to how adequately you can inform all interviewees about all these aspects. You need to think carefully about what to tell your interviewees when you are informing them. How much can and should you tell them, at what level of detail, complexity and sophistication, and at what points during the interaction? Many interviewees may not be very interested in the detail, and may not be familiar with the disciplinary and academic skills and conventions which are needed to understand issues about what counts as data, what principles of analysis will be used and so on. You may not be sure yourself, at this stage, about exactly how you will constitute and use your data, and about how you will use them to explain your intellectual puzzle. However, these limits mean that researchers need to take the issue of informed consent more rather than less seriously, in ensuring that they adopt an ethical form of practice. There are no easy answers or prescriptions about what that practice should be. But in my view, it is not sufficient simply to assert that you have gained informed consent because people have agreed to be interviewed, and you can therefore do what you want with the data and the analysis, if there are in fact some ambiguities in relation to the difficult questions outlined above. It may be impossible to receive a consent which is fully informed, and the responsible researcher should be prepared to recognize this, and think through its implications, in their research practice.

CONCLUSION

This chapter has examined some of the difficult questions which are raised by the use of qualitative interviewing. Perhaps the most important message is that this kind of interviewing is not an easy option, contrary to the view that such interviews are little more than everyday conversations which 'anyone could do'. Although interviewing can be rewarding and fascinating, I have also wanted to make it clear that qualitative interviewing is difficult intellectually, practically, socially and ethically, and that any researcher should be aware of the kind of challenge they are taking on in choosing to use this method. Furthermore, this kind of interviewing is greedy of resources: it is heavily consuming of skills, time and effort, both in the planning and conducting of the interviews themselves, and in the analysis of the products (which is discussed in Chapters 6 and 7).

All of this means that the decision to use qualitative interviewing should not be made lightly. It is, in fact, one of the most – possibly *the* most – widely used methods in qualitative research, and for some very good reasons. It is considered by many to be an appropriate and practicable way to get at some of what qualitative researchers see as the central ontological components of social reality. And that really is the key to the central issue in the choice of qualitative interviewing, or indeed any other method: it is absolutely crucial that there is a logic – based on sound ontological and epistemological principles, and tied into specific research questions – to that choice, and that it is a logic which guides the practice of interviewing, and the process of analysis.

FURTHER READING

Burgess, R.G. (1984) *In the Field: an Introduction to Field Research*, London: Allen and Unwin (Chapter 2)

Burgess, R.G. (1988) 'Conversations with a Purpose: the Ethnographic Interview in Educational Research' in R. G. Burgess (ed.) *Studies in Qualitative Methodology*, vol. 1, JAI Press

Denzin, N.K. (1989) *The Research Act: a Theoretical Introduction to Sociological Methods*, 3rd edn, New Jersey: Prentice Hall (Chapter 4)

Douglas, J.D. (1985) *Creative Interviewing*, London: Sage

Fontana, A. and Frey, J.H. (1994) 'Interviewing: the Art of Science' in N.K. Denzin and Y.S. Lincoln (eds) *Handbook of Qualitative Research*, London: Sage

Hammersley, M. and Atkinson, P. (1995) *Ethnography: Principles in Practice*, 2nd edn, London: Routledge

Silverman, D. (1985) *Qualitative Methodology and Sociology*, Aldershot: Gower (Chapter 8)

4
GENERATING QUALITATIVE DATA: OBSERVATION, DOCUMENTS AND VISUAL DATA

In the previous chapter we examined in some detail the use of qualitative interviewing to generate data, and the difficult questions with which researchers using that method should engage. We spent some time on each of the questions, since many of them can usefully be asked in relation to a wide range of data generating methods. In this chapter, we are going to take a briefer look at some other approaches to generating qualitative data, using the framework established in the previous chapter. We will begin with a consideration of another method which has a long standing association with qualitative research: observation. We will then go on to examine the use and generation of documents and of visual data. Throughout the chapter it will become clear that there are overlaps and intersections between different methods, and the concluding discussion will focus on some of the key issues involved in using multiple methods.

OBSERVATION: LOGIC AND RATIONALE

The term 'observation', and in particular 'participant observation', is usually used to refer to methods of generating data which involve the researcher immersing herself or himself in a research setting, and systematically observing dimensions of that setting, interactions, relationships, actions, events and so on, within it. Many of the texts on qualitative methods devote a great deal of attention to these observational methods, and in particular to the participant–observer dimension. There has been much debate about how far researchers should and can participate in the situations they study, and conversely whether it is possible or desirable simply to observe without participation (Burgess, 1982; 1984; Hammersley and Atkinson, 1995). For the moment, I am using the term 'observation' to refer to any kind of observational method, whether or not the researcher employing it thinks themselves to be simultaneously participating.

There is a long tradition of observational research in the social sciences, especially amongst those researchers influenced by social anthropology; hence the common use of the term 'ethnography' or 'field research' to describe the kind of research strategy which views observational methods as a central plank. Whether or not you locate yourself as a researcher within the anthropological or ethnographic tradition, you should begin by asking yourself the following question about observational methods:

> Why might I want to use
> observational methods?

As with the example of qualitative interviewing discussed in the previous chapter, I do not think you should expect your answers to be easy or simple. However, as well as needing to think through the intellectual logic behind the use of observation, it is also crucial to recognize that conducting observational research can be very time and resource consuming. You need to be sure of your reasons for doing it before making a major commitment. Here are some possible reasons why you might want to use observation as a method of data generation.

● You have an *ontological* perspective which sees interactions, actions and behaviours and the way people interpret these, act on them, and so on, as central. You may be interested in interactions involving large numbers of people (for example a mass demonstration, shopping in a town centre). You may be interested in a range of dimensions of the social world (for example, not just written responses to a questionnaire, or verbal responses to an interview, or written texts), including daily routines, conversations, language and rhetoric used, styles of behaviour (including non-verbal behaviour), the active construction of documents and texts in certain settings, and so on. You may be interested in interactions which take place in a certain context, and you may – in the long standing tradition of social anthropology – want to conceptualize these as interactions in their 'natural' settings. You may indeed be primarily interested in the setting itself, for example a pub or café, a town or 'community', a stock exchange, a music festival, a conference or meeting, a shopping centre, a classroom, a court of law, a hospital or clinic. If your ontological perspective encapsulates these kinds of ideas, you nevertheless do need to engage with criticisms of the idea that a setting can be natural once a researcher is involved.

● You have an *epistemological* position which suggests that knowledge or evidence of the social world can be generated by observing, or participating in, or experiencing 'natural' or 'real life' settings, interactive situations and so on. Such a position is based on the premise that these kinds of settings, situations and interactions 'reveal data', and also that it is possible for a researcher to be an interpreter or 'knower' of such data as well as an experiencer, observer, or a participant observer. Indeed, many devotees of observation would argue that the researcher can be a 'knower' in these circumstances precisely because of shared experience, participation or a shared 'standpoint' with the researched. In other words, they know what the experience of that social setting feels like, although of course not necessarily from the perspective of all participants and actors involved, and in that sense they are epistemologically privileged. Whether or not you accept this notion of epistemological privilege, at the very least, you will probably hold the view that observation allows the generation of data on social interaction in specific contexts as it occurs, rather than relying on people's retrospective accounts, and on their ability to verbalize and reconstruct a version of interactions. You may regard such situationally generated data as superior, or as simply different from a *post hoc* reconstruction. You must, nevertheless, take on board criticisms of the simplistic 'standpoint' position – that is, that you are a 'knower' because you share relevant experiences, or because you have 'been there' – especially in so far as you cannot assume that your experience of a setting, and your social location and so on, match those of all others involved.

- Your view of the ways in which *social explanations* can be constructed – in common with advocates of qualitative interviewing – lays emphasis on depth, complexity and roundedness in data, rather than surface analysis of broad patterns, or direct comparisons of 'like with like' (such as the comparison of interviewee responses to a standardized set of questions). It is likely also to lay some emphasis on 'naturally' or situationally occurring data, rather than data which are clearly artificially manufactured or manipulated through, for example, experimental research design, or possibly even through the use of questionnaires and interviews. Again, as with qualitative interviewing, you are likely to build explanations through some form of grounded and interpretive data analysis, and you may place little emphasis on enumeration. You will nevertheless find yourself having to engage with some very powerful criticisms of explanations based on observational methods: namely, that they are subjective, unrepresentative and ungeneralizable.

- You are highly likely to conceptualize *yourself as active and reflexive* in the research process, not least because of the premium placed on the experiential nature of this form of data generation. Most users of observational methods write themselves into their fieldnotes. Of course you must not underestimate the challenge of analysing your own role in this way.

- Your assessment is that the kind of *data you require are not available in other forms* or ways. For example, this may be because your view is that retrospective accounts of interactions are inadequate or impossible to achieve.

- You may use observation as *one of several methods* to explore your research questions, although as with qualitative interviewing, you will need to think carefully about the implications of and possibilities for integration of methods. It is worth pointing out that many researchers who do some form of observation actually use a range of other methods and techniques as part of the process. So, for example, it is common for an observer to conduct interviews with key participants – sometimes spontaneously, sometimes in a planned way – or to use or generate documents or visual data.

- You may feel it is more *ethical* to enter into and become involved in the social world of those you research to gain your understandings, than to attempt to 'stand outside' by using other methods. You must, however, be conversant with debates about the ethics of covert and overt observation, and about the merits of adopting different roles on the participant–observer continuum, and be prepared to take some difficult decisions about these issues. Observation is rarely viewed or experienced by researchers as an ethically straightforward or easy method.

PLANNING AND CARRYING OUT OBSERVATION

If you are intending to enter a setting, situation or interaction, to carry out some form of observation, then you will need to prepare yourself not just for the process and technique of observance, but also for social interaction. You will be variously involved in observing, participating, interrogating, listening, communicating, as well as a range of other forms of being, doing and thinking. This means that all of the points made in the previous chapter about managing and orchestrating social interactions apply here also. You are likely to find the process more challenging and exhausting than conducting interviews because settings, situations and interaction can be notoriously messy and compli-cated, with lots of things happening at once; your own role may be less clear cut than if you are an 'interviewer', and subject to frequent negotiation and renegotiation; and you may involve yourself in your setting for lengthy periods of time. If the social dynamics present a major challenge, so too do the intellectual issues involved in generating data from settings, situations and interactions. You must, therefore, ask yourself some very difficult questions about observation to ensure that you not only prepare yourself as fully as possible in advance, but also continue to take informed and strategic decisions throughout the whole process of data generation. Here are some examples of key questions – at the very least you need to work out your answers to these, and for most of them you will need to do this before, during and after the process of data generation:

> Do I intend to be a participant, an observer, or a participant-observer?

At its simplest, the answer to this question requires you to select a role on the continuum between complete participant and complete observer, and to understand the implications of your selection for the research process and its products. However, this is not a simple selection to make – especially not in the abstract – and what is more you may find that you do not take a 'once and for all' decision about this, but in fact that you move between a variety of roles in any one research project for both intellectual and practical reasons (see Burgess, 1984). To begin with, you should ask yourself how far it is possible to be a complete observer, in the sense that you have no influence on the setting, or that your observations remain 'untainted' by experiencing or feeling what the setting is like. For many enthusiasts of the method, this notion of researcher distance or neutrality is not only impossible, but completely defeats the epistemological purpose of immersing yourself in a setting. In other words, you are – according to this view – supposed to know what it feels like rather than simply act as a detached witness. But you should of course also ask yourself how far it is possible to be a participant. There are likely to be various answers to this depending, in part, on what you understand by the term 'participation'. One view is that you cannot fail to participate in some form, and the problem is that you cannot control how your participation is perceived by others. For example, if you try to be nonparticipative, or neutral in your expressed views and actions, this may be interpreted in a whole range of ways by those involved – the point being that it will be *interpreted* and *responded to* in some way. Your attempts at lack of involvement in whatever is going on in the setting will have some effects and cannot be judged to be the same as if you were simply absent from the setting altogether. So, if you cannot be a 'fly on the wall', can you participate in such a way that you effectively understand the setting *because* you are part of it? In other words, can you gain epistemological privilege by participating in and experiencing what is going on? There are problems here too, and you must ask yourself to what extent you are really in the same position, or have the same perspective, as everyone else in the setting: are there some divisions, or differences of perspective or interest, between you and 'them', and between 'them'? The answer is almost certainly yes, and your job will be to try to understand the basis of those divisions. These difficulties do not mean that you should remain undecided about your participant or observer status. Instead, they mean that you should keep it constantly in focus.

> What kind(s) of identity(ies), status or role(s) do I wish to adopt? What impression should I try to create?

This is an extension of the first question, in that whatever answer you give will almost certainly influence your positioning on the participant–observer continuum. It also carries similar difficulties, in the sense that you may be unable to control the ways in which your identity, status or role are perceived, and you may find yourself constantly trying to negotiate and renegotiate them. You will need to decide whether you admit your status as a researcher, for example. Whilst most ethical codes would suggest that you should not conduct research in a covert or deceitful manner, and there have been extensive debates about the merits of covert or overt observation in the social sciences, you may find that an overt role is not always easy or possible to maintain. For example, if your setting is a busy pub, or a railway station, how can you feasibly inform everyone of your status? Even in small groups, it is not always possible to preface every interaction or meeting with a few well chosen words about your role as a researcher. You may of course take on other roles in your setting: you might join a factory as an assembly line worker, a school as a teacher, a club as a member, and so on. You will need to think about the implications of your role(s) for data generation and for your ability to move around in the setting. So, for example, a teacher clearly gets a rather specific perspective on classroom interaction. You will also need to think about the practicalities of adopting such a role: are you trained, can you perform the role adequately, will other characteristics – for example your age, your gender, your ethnicity – influence your ability to take on the role? And there are of course other less formal aspects of your identity, status or role which you should think about. For example, what kind of demeanour are you going to adopt in your setting, and in different situations? How are you going to behave? Are you going to be accommodating, aggressive, reticent, garrulous? What impression are you going to try to create? I am not suggesting that you can or should plan all of this in advance, and then simply act out a script. But at the very least you should think about these issues in advance, and try continually to be aware of them and to understand their relevance in the interactions, situations and settings you are studying.

> How do I decide on the location, the situation or the setting? Where is what I am interested in located – in time, space and place?

Locating a context or setting in or from which you will be able to generate data relevant to your research questions can be quite challenging intellectually as well as practically. Intellectually, it requires you to think carefully about what is your intellectual puzzle, and what phenomena you are attempting to investigate. Then you need to think about where these might be located in time, space and place. So, for example, if you are interested in the concept of community, you must think about where communities are located according to these dimensions. If you focus on 'public' settings such as shops, cafés, post offices, parks, and so on, at certain times of day or year, are you overlooking a central aspect of community which might be located in more 'private' places, such as people's households, or less tangible 'places' such as telephone conversations, or which might be activated at different times? Practical issues will arise in connection with whether your setting is feasibly and physically accessible, which leads to the next question.

> Can I gain access to the setting? What does access really mean?

You may wish to gain access to a setting which is 'public', such as the examples of railways stations and pubs given above. In these cases, access may seem fairly unproblematic. However, you will need to think about how far you can gain access to all the dimensions which you are interested in, because even apparently public settings are likely to contain regions or interactions which are out of bounds to the general public. You may also need to negotiate access as a researcher – rather than as a passenger, client or customer – to these types of settings. Where settings are obviously 'private' in some way you will need to negotiate access with the relevant gatekeepers but again, as with public settings, you should not assume that access is either granted or denied universally to your setting. You must continue to use your critical judgement to assess what kind of access you have – for example it might be full, partial, conditional, intermittent – and to which regions or interactions. In negotiating access, and in trying to work out just what kind of access you have been granted, you will be focusing upon forming relationships with others in the setting.

> How should I go about developing relationships in the setting? How can I gain acceptance? How will I know whether I have been accepted?

Developing relationships in your setting can be very difficult, and the way you do this is likely to have significant implications for the kind of access you actually achieve. The development of relationships in your setting will, at least in part, be governed by a range of social norms. So, for example, if you are observing in a pub or a railway station, certain kinds of sociability and relationship building may seem more appropriate to some participants than others. You may risk being seen as over-friendly, or intrusive, or suspicious, or threatening, if you approach strangers for a chat in these settings. Aspects of your demeanour, and ascribed characteristics such as your gender, will have a bearing here also. Whatever the setting, it is inevitable that the researcher will get on better with some participants than others, and may actually be 'adopted' by a 'key informant' who might then introduce them to other people or regions in the setting. The advantages and disadvantages of using key informants are well documented in the literature on participant observation (Burgess, 1982; 1984; Hammersley and Atkinson, 1995). Chiefly, you will need to think about the implications of using any one key informant. So, for example, in an organizational setting, would it matter if your key informant was an unpopular manager, a trade union representative, a woman who had made a formal complaint about being sexually harassed by a colleague? Would your relationship with this person affect your standing and credibility (and therefore access to certain interactions and regions) with other members of the organization? Whether or not you identify a key informant, it is unrealistic to assume that you can maintain a completely neutral stance in the development of relationships in your setting, and so you must think through the implications of forming specific alliances. You must ask yourself whether you have gained 'acceptance' from all of those involved, and what exactly that acceptance might mean. Your answers to such questions will of course be tentative, since you simply will not always – or ever – be in a position to know how others see you, but you should ensure that you continue to analyse yourself, and your interactions with others, so that you can make judgements about these issues.

All of this needs to be taking place alongside the more obvious intellectual questions about observation, specifically:

> What am I looking for in the setting?

> How do I generate data within the setting? Where do the data come from?

Although the purpose of observation is to witness what is going on in a particular setting or set of interactions, the intellectual problem for the researcher is what to observe and what to be interested in. If you reject the view – as I do – that it is possible to produce a full and neutral account of a setting or set of interactions based on observation, then you must work out how to tackle the questions of selectivity and perspective in observation, since any observation is inevitably going to be selective, and to be based upon a particular observational perspective. The key to this is to try to understand *how* you are using selectivity and perspective, rather than to assume – or to hope – that you are not. This means that you must have at least some sense of what you are looking for in the setting, and some critical awareness of how that has informed what you have observed, and what you have found interesting and relevant. You should, therefore, prepare yourself quite carefully in an intellectual sense before you begin your observation, and you can use procedures like those detailed in the previous chapter for preparing for interviews. As discussed there, you will need a procedure for linking your research questions to questions you might ask, or observations you might be able to make, in the 'field'. Whilst your procedure for doing this is likely to be more fluid, and more ongoing, than that for qualitative interviews, you must nevertheless have some kind of procedure to help you to make situated yet strategic decisions – for example about what to look for next, whom to speak with next, what to record in some way and follow up – once you are observing in your setting. The research community is perhaps rather too populated by researchers who overestimated their ability simply to 'hang around' in a setting or location and to 'soak up' relevant data. As well as the intellectual issues involved in working out what you are interested in, and how to handle selectivity and perspective, this raises more practical methodological issues about how to ensure that relevant data are generated during your time in the field. Simply 'hanging around' in an unfocused way can be notoriously time consuming and unproductive. You will need to consider how you will generate data, or how you will ensure that you are in the right place at the right time to collect data and make meaningful observations. You may wish to use other data generation methods alongside observation. For example, you may conduct some interviews, or at least invite some of those involved in the setting to reflect on their understandings and experiences. You may collect or generate some documentary or visual data, for example you might take photographs, draw maps and diagrams of spatial locations and events, collect newspaper reports about your setting, and so on.

Whilst you will certainly wish to take decisions about these kinds of issues in an ongoing way as your research progresses, you must also ensure that you do think quite extensively about them in advance of entering your observational setting so that you are maximizing your intellectual and practical resources.

TURNING OBSERVATIONS INTO DATA

In the previous chapter we examined some of the processes qualitative researchers should go through in order to transform interview interactions into what they consider to be data. These questions, about what count as data, how you produce and recognize data, and construct them in a form which you can analyse or systematize in some way, apply with equal resonance to observational methods. In fact, the issues often appear more complex in relation to observation, because the researcher may be forming impressions and developing interpretations on the basis of a more variable and sometimes less tangible range of interfaces with the social world – it can all feel much more vague, fluid and arbitrary. Therefore, it is vital that those using observational methods ask themselves all of the difficult questions which qualitative interviewers should ask about how to generate data from their method, and in particular that they should pay attention to how they wish to handle the distinction between *literal*, *interpretive* and *reflexive* 'readings' (see Chapter 3). Additionally, there are several more pertinent questions which observers should ask themselves, as follows:

> How and when should I record my observations? What should I record?

The 'how' questions about recording observations are similar to those for qualitative interviewing, in the sense that you will need to make decisions about whether to make notes while you are observing, to write up 'fieldnotes' at some point following your observations, whether to use other aids like video or audio tapes, photography, diagrams and charts, and so on. These decisions must be taken in the context of grounded critical judgements about what each can offer in relation to your research and its context, and what the limitations are, and you should retain a healthy scepticism, as discussed in Chapter 3, about the 'objectivity' and totality of some apparently literal methods like audio and video recording. You will need to think about the form of the data produced by the different recording methods, and about what kinds of subsequent analyses will therefore be possible. Your decisions will also be influenced by practical matters such as what recording methods are possible in the setting (for example, audio recording may not work very well in very noisy settings, or may be forbidden), and what your role allows you to do (for example an assembly line worker may have little opportunity to make notes or a video whilst observing). If you have taken the contentious decision to perform covert observation, then some of the more obtrusive methods of simultaneous recording will not be available to you. And of course your chosen method(s) will have an influence on your setting and the interactions within it, just as your own presence does. So, for example, your presence and role may be interpreted variously depending upon whether you view everything through your camcorder, whether you keep breaking off conversations to make jottings in your notebook, whether you are taking photographs, and so on.

Your chosen method of recording will of course influence what you are able to record. So, for example, a video recording will give you visual images and possibly a soundtrack, but will not say anything about your own interpretations of the setting, your feelings about what was happening, and so on. Of course many observers use more than one method of recording, and most make fieldnotes or a field diary of some kind, which records their observations and interpretations in a more or less reflexive manner. Given the premium placed on the experiential nature of observation, it is vital to ensure that whatever data recording methods you are using they do help you to observe, record and analyse your own role in and experience of the setting and its interactions. In my view fieldnotes are essential for this purpose, whether or not you use other methods as well. Remember that if you are behind a camcorder making a video recording, you will not also be in the picture. Substantive issues about what you record, in the sense of what themes you choose to write about in your fieldnotes, or where you choose to point your camera or your microphone, must be tied in with your research questions, or your intellectual puzzle, which means you must have a self-conscious sense of 'what it is you really want to know about', whilst you are observing and recording. Your preparation in answer to the earlier question 'what am I looking for in the setting?' will help you here and, as with qualitative interviewing, it needs to be a form of preparation which allows you to be innovative and flexible in your vision when you are in the field, rather than blinkering you by imposing a very rigid set of preconceptions. It is worth reiterating, however, that you will be being naive if you think you can produce a complete or literal description of your setting and that therefore you do not have to prepare to 'look for' anything at all. You will inevitably be making a record of your observations which is structured around certain themes, issues and interests. It is therefore imperative that you are clear about what those interests are, as well as how and why you are recording observations around them.

ETHICAL ISSUES IN OBSERVATION

Many of the debates about the ethics of qualitative research have taken place around the issue of observation and, in particular, the question of whether covert observation can in any circumstances be regarded as ethically acceptable (see especially Bulmer, 1982; also Homan, 1991). Whilst the choice of covert or overt observation clearly is an important issue, this should not overshadow the overt observer's engagement with the more 'ordinary' range of ethical matters discussed in relation to qualitative interviewing (see Chapter 3). So, for example, questions about the ethics of your overall research practice and where you derive your ethical position from, or questions about the way in which you build and maintain relationships in the field, the power dynamics which operate and your role in them, the issue of informed consent and your rights over the data and analysis, are all central in the practice of observation. Some are raised in particularly sharp form such as, for example, the gaining of informed consent which can be very difficult to achieve – even for the overt observer – in a complex and multi-faceted social setting.

DOCUMENTS AND VISUAL DATA: LOGIC AND RATIONALE

The analysis of documentary sources is a major method of social research, and one which many qualitative researchers see as meaningful and appropriate in the context of their research strategy. The idea of documentary research tends to conjure up a mental image of a researcher digging around in a dusty archive amongst historical documents, but in fact there are many different ways of generating data through documents, and many different types of documents. Some documents exist already, prior to the act of research upon them. Others can be generated for or through the research process. Some examples of the first type are: Acts of Parliament; Congressional papers; insurance policies; bank statements; accounts and balance sheets; company reports; wills; minutes of meetings; books, manuals and other publications; diaries; letters; shopping lists; computer files and documents; newspapers and magazines; rough notes and scribbles; menus; advertisements. Some examples of documents which can be generated for or through the research process are: diaries; time diaries; written accounts and stories; biographies; charts, tables and lists. Such documents can be generated by you as the researcher, or you can ask people or bodies you are researching to generate them for or with you.

All of these examples are text-based documents, although many of them will also contain non-text-based elements which may be of interest to the researcher (for example the graphics and layout of newspapers and magazines). Documents are usually considered to be text-based, but they are not necessarily so, and some commentators will include non-text-based documents – especially photographs – in their discussions of documentary methods (see for example Plummer, 1983; Scott, 1990). Other non-text-based forms of data sit less comfortably under the heading of 'documents', and there are less clearly established conventions for using them in social science research (see Ball and Smith, 1992 for a good review). Examples of these are film, video and television, displays, graphic representations, sculpture, drawings and pictures, visual art and artefacts, style and fashion, diagrams, 'cognitive maps' (that is, diagrams which attempt to map out such things as thought processes, or sets of social interactions) and so on. The same distinction – between data generated for or through the research process, and those already in existence – applies to these forms of visual data. So, for example, you may conduct an analysis of a particular genre of film, or you may produce pictures and cognitive maps jointly with your interviewees. Because they do not take a text-based form, we *have to* think about visual, spatial and design elements of such data, but it should be recognized that such elements may well be of relevance to researchers using other methods, as well as to text-based forms of data. In other words, the visual 'gaze' should not be confined to the generation and use of wholly visual data.

Indeed, some overlap between documentary and visual methods on the one hand, and other methods of data generation on the other, should be noted here because as well as using such techniques alongside, for example, interviewing and observation, a researcher may very well produce documents such as fieldnotes and transcripts, or visual data such as video and film, for analysis *as part of* these methods. We have seen that the idea that observations and interviews become *data* when they are transformed into text is a very influential one in the social sciences. This probably has the effect of overemphasizing the inherent credibility of documentary data, and underplaying that of visual and other non-text-based forms of data. The implication is that text has a superior or concrete and indisputable quality, but you should not uncritically accept such a claim about *any* document – whether or not you yourself produced it. Instead, you should ensure that you subject all documents, including those you have produced, to exactly the same degree of critical scrutiny. And of course you should do the same with non-documentary visual data.

As with all other methods of data generation, the first question you should ask yourself in relation to documentary methods and visual data is why you might want to use them:

> Why might I want to use or generate text-based and/or non-text-based documents?

> Why might I want to use or generate other forms of visual data?

Briefly, here are some possible answers:

- You have an *ontological* position which suggests that written words, texts, documents, records, visual or spatial phenomena or aspects of social organization, shape, form, and so on, are meaningful constituents of the social world in themselves (you may see them as more meaningful than, for example, verbal utterances), or you may be interested in the processes by which they are produced or consumed, or you may believe that they act as some form of expression or representation of relevant elements of the social world, or that we can trace or 'read' aspects of the social world through them.

- You have an *epistemological* position which suggests that words, texts, documents, written records, visual documents, visual records, visual artefacts and phenomena, can provide or count as evidence of these ontological properties. This might be in a literal sense – for example they *are* the evidence, or they straightforwardly reflect evidence – or in a more interpretive sense – for example they need to be read and interpreted for evidence. It is tempting, as suggested above, to see documents as providing 'hard' or especially legitimate evidence, but your epistemology should be more critical than this, and you should exercise a high degree of sophistication and scepticism in the reading and interpretation of documents just as you would with visual images.

- Data on the phenomena you are interested in may simply *not be available in other forms*. For example, you may be interested in historical events to which there are no living witnesses, but which are documented in some form, or related to which visual images exist. Alternatively, you may be unable to find anyone appropriate to interview, or unable to locate a 'field' or 'setting' to enter. Documents or visual data may provide a way of gaining access to, for example, a set of events or processes, which you cannot observe (for example because they have already occurred, because they take place in private) without recourse to verbal descriptions and reconstructions. If you see texts or visual and spatial images as ontologically meaningful in themselves, then your corresponding epistemological position may be that these simply cannot be 'known' or captured in other media, such as verbal descriptions.

- You may wish to use documents or visual data *alongside several other methods* of data generation. Sometimes, documents are used to verify or contextualize or clarify personal recollections and other forms of data derived from, for example, interviewing and observation. You might construct visual images and accounts, or examine visual data and artefacts, as well as conducting interviews and observations. You may actively use documents or visual data in interviews and observations. For example, you might ask people their responses to a set of photographs, or you might ask them to read and comment on a document. Documents and visual data may provide an alternative angle on, or add another dimension to, your research questions. Remember, however, that the integration of different methods is not an entirely straightforward matter, and you will need to revisit the questions posed in Chapter 2 about how you might integrate, and what you are expecting to achieve in so doing.

- Relevant documents or visual data exist. This is a pragmatic answer to the question, implying as it does that you might use documents or visual data *because they are there*. You may know that relevant documents or visual data exist, or that you can gain easy access to them, and this may drive your decision to use them. Certainly, research based on the use of already existing documents and visual data needs to work itself, and its intellectual puzzle, around what is there and what is possible, and it is probably fair to say that much historical research begins with an assessment of the range of documents available, and then goes on to ask what kinds of research questions it might be possible to address on this basis. However, although in these cases the process of linking questions to methods may occur in a different sequence, there is no less need to ensure that the decisions taken about data sources and method are systematic and strategic. At the very least, you would not wish to use documents or visual data – whether or not they exist and are easy to access – if your ontological position suggests they represent nothing meaningful about the social world, or your epistemological position says that they do not count as evidence. You might also not wish to use them if they are only tangentially relevant, and you should be aware that scrutinizing large numbers of documents, or a wide range of types of visual data, can be very time and labour intensive, as well as intellectually challenging.

COLLECTING AND GENERATING DOCUMENTS AND VISUAL DATA

The generation and use of documents and visual data do not inherently involve the researcher in social interactions as do interviewing and observation, although of course they may do. If in that sense the preparation for using these methods seems simpler, there are nevertheless some distinctive issues raised by them, and we shall consider some of the most important ones. Chiefly, these involve asking yourself critical questions about the nature of the sources you are using or generating, as well as questions about what it is you want from them, or expect to be able to get from them.

> What do I really want to know, and can documents or visual data tell me about this?

Just as a qualitative interviewer or observer needs to be forearmed with a good sense of what they are looking for, so too does the researcher using documents or visual images. Anyone who has fulfilled the stereotype of spending lengthy periods in a dusty archive will confirm this. It is little use spending six months reading documents, and then deciding at the end of that period what it is you were looking for. You will need to begin by asking yourself what you expect documents or visual data to be able to tell you about, in an ontological and epistemological sense, and in particular to consider which parts of your intellectual puzzle they might potentially help you to address. You will furthermore need to think carefully about *how* you expect them to do this, and this will relate to the issue of how you expect to be able to 'read' your documents or visual data. For example, do you expect them to tell you in a literal sense about the phenomena you are interested in – perhaps because they *are* the phenomena you are interested in, or because you are interested in their literal form, construction and content? Or do you expect to 'read' them for something else – you might see them as representations of something else, or as the textual or visual manifestations of cultural discourses, or you might expect to be able to infer something about underlying societal rules, practices, norms or mechanisms on their basis?

You must work out the answers to these questions, so that you can develop a clear set of principles for dealing with selectivity and perspective in your handling of documents and visual data. As I suggested in relation to both observation, and interviewing, you will inevitably be operating in a way which both is selective and uses a particular perspective, and you need to be clear and consistent about how you do this. Just as with those other methods, you should develop a technique or mechanism for ensuring that you are doing this, and to help you to be systematic in recording what you have scrutinized.

> How do I assess the value and productive potential for my research of documents and visual data? How should I decide which ones to use?

You will need to ask this question in relation to the specific documents and visual data which are available, or which you can generate, rather than in the abstract. You should consider the following:

- What level of detail or fullness is provided by the documents or visual data?

- How complete an account or perspective will they provide? Do I need other forms of data, or other contextual information, to make sense of them?

- Why were they prepared, made or displayed, by whom, for whom, under what conditions, according to what rules and conventions? What have they been used for?

- Are they authentic and genuine? Are they reliable and accurate?

You may not know the answers to all of these questions, but you will need to get as far as you can with them as they will help you to situate the documents or visual data in the context of their nature, production and use. These factors will influence how valuable and productive such documents and visual data can be in the context of your own requirements, which you will have specified in your answer to the previous question. As Scott points out in his excellent text on documentary sources:

> Textual analysis involves mediation between the frames of reference of the researcher and those who produced the text. The aim of this dialogue is to move within the 'hermeneutic circle' in which we comprehend a text by understanding that frame of reference from which it was produced, and appreciate that frame of reference by understanding the text. The researcher's own frame of reference becomes the springboard from which the circle is entered, and so the circle reaches back to encompass the dialogue between the researcher and the text. (1990: 32)

The next questions are more practical:

> Do appropriate documents or visual data exist, and can I gain access to them? Or can I generate appropriate documentary or visual data?

As I stated earlier, many documentary researchers actually begin with these types of questions, since their intellectual puzzles sometimes have to be shaped around the availability of documentary evidence. But of course any researcher contemplating using documents or visual data should engage with such questions, and should set to work on the logistics of gaining access to the relevant materials. It is important to bear in mind the full range of practicalities here: for example, the relevant documents or visual images may well exist, but they may be so numerous, or so badly filed, or so disparate, as to make systematic retrieval and analysis of them very difficult to achieve without unlimited financial and temporal resources. You may want to gain access to only a small number of documents, but be unable to find what you want amongst an amorphous and messy bulk. You will need to work out the feasibility of doing what you want, and the value of what the documents or visual data can provide for your project in that context.

TURNING DOCUMENTS AND THE VISUAL INTO DATA

When you first begin to engage with the question of how you turn your documents or your visual images into data it may seem as though the task is simplest in relation to text-based documents. After all, there is a strong tendency amongst qualitative researchers to think of data as text, and the fact that text-based documents *already* take a textual form makes them look more like data than, for example, a film or a painting. However, such an assumption is based solely on the idea of a literal 'reading' of text-based documents; when you begin to ask yourself the difficult questions about what count as data which were explored in Chapter 3 in relation to qualitative interviewing, a wider range of ways of deriving data from text-based documents becomes possible.

> What count as data in documents and visual images? Do I wish to 'read' them in a literal, interpretive or reflexive sense?

- You may wish to view the text of a text-based document, in a *literal* sense, as data.

- You may wish to include *other literal elements* of text-based documents apart from the text – for example visual, layout and design elements – in your understanding of what count as data.

- You may wish to include *interpretive* elements of text-based documents – for example factors relevant to or speaking of their context, production and consumption – in your understanding of what count as data.

- Not all of the text-based elements contained in the documents will necessarily be meaningful to you as data.

- You may wish to see other aspects of your interface with the documents – in a *reflexive* sense – as data.

This means that text-based documents should not be read only in a literal or simplistic sense *as* data in themselves, and that you should maintain the same degree of critical awareness about what count as data in their context as you would for interviews, observations and indeed visual images. Indeed, looked at in this way, the derivation of data from text-based documents looks no more easy than from visual images, since for both you will be making critical judgements about how and why various elements – literal, interpretive and reflexive – might represent data. The difference is simply that visual images themselves, in a literal sense, may contain no text whatsoever. The answer to the next question will be driven by your answers to these difficult ones about what count as data.

> What should I collect or record? How should I record it?

Once you have moved past the point where you view documents or visual images as simply data in themselves, you will begin to think about what it is that you want to take from them in the process of deriving data. This may mean taking, or copying, whole documents or images for subsequent analysis, but it may also mean that you will select elements of them, record specific things about them (for example, this might be literal quotations from a document, or it might be written or visual notes about form, style and structure in visual images). You will clearly need to think carefully about what you expect from the literal, interpretive and reflexive dimensions, so that you can make certain that you collect and record in relevant ways. For example, if you are interested in literal wording, form and sequence in a text-based document, then you will need to devise a literal method of recording these. If you are interested in the location of a painting in an art gallery, and in the ways in which viewers respond to it, then you will need to record something other than the literal form and style of the painting. You might make maps and diagrams, count numbers of viewers, take photographs, make written fieldnotes. These strategies in their turn will produce forms of text- and non-text-based data for further analysis. Make sure you consider the practicalities of your choices of recording strategy. For example, is it possible or desirable to make photocopies of all the documents you wish to analyse? Can you afford to do this, in terms of time and money? Will you be permitted to do this by the owners or keepers of the documents, by copyright legislation, and so on?

ETHICAL ISSUES IN THE USE OF DOCUMENTS AND VISUAL DATA

Ethical issues can feel less immediate for researchers using documents and visual data, because they may be involved in fewer face-to-face interactions than interviewers and observers. However, documents and visual data can take a very private or confidential form, and it can be difficult to establish informed consent for their use because they may refer to or implicate people other than their owners or keepers. You may feel that the person or body who is able to give you permission to use a set of documents does not actually have the moral authority to grant such use. Therefore, all the questions about ethical practice and informed consent apply equally to the use of documents and visual data. You may need to think quite carefully about whether or not you wish to, and should, reproduce documents and visual images in your data analysis. So, for example, if you are conducting a study of pornography and the exploitation of women, and you are collecting visual images for your research, you will have to confront the issue of whether – if you reproduce them – you are collaborating in the process of exploitation. If you are generating your own documents or visual images, you will need to scrutinize the ethics of this kind of production, especially in relation to whether you have gained or can gain the informed consent of everyone involved. (Ethical issues in the analysis of qualitative data are discussed more fully in Chapter 7.)

CONCLUSION: USING MULTIPLE METHODS

In this and the previous chapter we have considered three of the key methods of data generation used in qualitative research. I have not, of course, covered the whole range, nor have I said everything there is to say about each method. Instead, I have focused on some of the key issues – and the types of thinking – with which you will need to engage when using each of the methods. It should be noted that the boundaries between the different methods can become quite blurred so that, for example, observation might involve the generation of visual data or the conducting of interviews. Furthermore, the difficult questions which you should ask yourself – although not always exactly the same for each method – have significant similarities and overlaps. There are good reasons for subjecting yourself to the discipline of asking a core of questions about every method which you use (or might use), and for this reason each method has been discussed using a similar framework.

As I have suggested, as well as using methods in ways which blur the edges between them, many researchers also wish explicitly to use multiple methods to address their research questions, and I would encourage such creative and lateral thinking about methodological choices and strategies. However, as suggested in Chapter 2, a researcher must think strategically about the integration of multiple methods, rather than piecing them together in an *ad hoc* and eclectic way. This means that, as well as asking all of the difficult questions about *each* method outlined in this and the previous chapter, you should also ask those questions about the *combination* of methods which you propose to employ. I will not reiterate the full set of questions here, but I will emphasize some key ones, as follows:

> What can each method yield in relation to my research questions? Which parts of the puzzle do they help me to address?

You will already have asked yourself this in relation to your research design (see Chapter 2), and you will ask it in relation to each method. But you also need to remember to keep this to the front of your mind whilst making decisions on all of the related questions about method, for example, what to record, what to ask next in an interview, and so on. You will need a sense of how you see the pieces of the puzzle fitting together in order to direct your strategic thinking and decisions about method during the whole research process.

> How do the different methods feed into each other? How do they integrate logistically as well as intellectually?

This question requires you to revisit all the difficult points about integration of method discussed in Chapter 2, but again it requires that you have these ideas clearly at the front of your mind when you are making ongoing decisions about method. So, for example, you may decide that the effective generation of data using one method, say interviews, is contingent upon your prior analysis of data from another method, say documents. Or you may think – for intellectual reasons – that it is important that two of your methods of data generation are conducted simultaneously. If so, you need to work out the logistics of doing this. Is it possible? In other words you will need to think through the practical implications of the kinds of integration of data and method you have in mind.

> How will I derive data from each method – literally, interpretively or reflexively?

You will have thought about this question for each of your methods, and it will direct your thinking on how you go about turning each method into data. However, if you are using more than one method then you need, again, to take an overview of your answers to this question, and make sure that each answer makes sense in relation to the next. For example, does it make sense only to derive data reflexively from your observations, but not from your interviews or visual images?

> Can I feasibly do everything I want to do?

This final question is designed to take you firmly back into the realm of practicality. You must address yourself to the question of whether you have or can develop sufficient resources – in terms of, for example, time, money, skills – to perform the whole package of data generation activities which you have in mind. This is particularly important for those using multiple methods, because you need to make sure you are taking account of the resources required to integrate those methods, as well as simply conducting the different bits. Of course, decisions about resources cannot be made until you know the range and scope of your enquiry. How *many* interviews do you wish to conduct? How *many* settings do you wish to observe? How *many* documents and visual images do you wish to examine? How *long* will it take you to select and gain access to your interviewees, settings, documents and images? These issues are at the heart of the process of sampling and selection, and it is to the difficult questions about these that we now turn.

FURTHER READING

On Observation

Adler, P.A. and Adler, P. (1994) 'Observational Techniques' in N. K. Denzin and Y. S. Lincoln (eds) *Handbook of Qualitative Research*, London: Sage
Atkinson, P. (1990) *The Ethnographic Imagination*, London: Routledge
Atkinson, P. (1992) *Understanding Ethnographic Texts*, London: Sage
Atkinson, P. and Hammersley, M. (1994) 'Ethnography and Participant Observation' in N.K. Denzin and Y.S. Lincoln (eds) *Handbook of Qualitative Research*, London: Sage
Bulmer, M. (ed.) (1982) *Social Research Ethics*, New York: Holmes and Meier
Burgess, R.G. (1982) *Field Research: a Sourcebook and Field Manual*, London: Allen and Unwin
Burgess, R.G. (1984) *In the Field: an Introduction to Field Research*, London: Allen and Unwin (Chapter 4)
Burgess, R.G. (ed.) (1990) *Studies in Qualitative Methodology*, vol. 2, JAI Press
Denzin, N.K. (1989) *The Research Act: a Theoretical Introduction to Sociological Methods*, 3rd edn, New Jersey: Prentice Hall (Chapter 7)
Fetterman, D. (1989) *Ethnography: Step by Step*, London: Sage
Hammersley, M. (1992) *What's Wrong with Ethnography?*, London: Routledge
Hammersley, M. and Atkinson, P. (1995) *Ethnography: Principles in Practice*, 2nd edn, London: Routledge
Lofland, J. and Lofland, L.H. (1984) *Analyzing Social Settings: a Guide to Qualitative Observation and Analysis*, 2nd edn, Belmont, CA: Wadsworth
Skeggs, B. (1994) 'Situating the Production of Feminist Ethnography' in M. Maynard and J. Purvis (eds) *Researching Women's Lives from a Feminist Perspective*, London: Taylor and Francis
Stacey, J. (1988) 'Can There Be a Feminist Ethnography?' *Women's Studies International Forum*, vol. 11, no. 1, pp. 21–7
Thomas, J. (1993) *Doing Critical Ethnography*, London: Sage

On Documents and Visual Data

Ball, M.S. and Smith, G.W.H. (1992) *Analyzing Visual Data*, London: Sage
Burgess, R.G. (1984) *In the Field: an Introduction to Field Research*, London: Allen and Unwin (Chapter 6)
Denzin, N.K. (1989) *The Research Act: a Theoretical Introduction to Sociological Methods*, 3rd edn, New Jersey: Prentice Hall (Chapter 9)

Harper, D. (1994) 'On the Authority of the Image: Visual Methods at the Crossroads' in N. K. Denzin and Y. S. Lincoln (eds) *Handbook of Qualitative Research*, London: Sage
Hockings, P. (ed.) (1975) *Principles of Visual Anthropology*, Mouton
Hodder, I. (1994) 'The Interpretation of Documents and Material Culture' in N.K. Denzin and Y.S. Lincoln (eds) *Handbook of Qualitative Research*, London: Sage
Platt, J. (1981) 'Evidence and Proof in Documentary Research' *Sociological Review*, vol. 29, no. 1, pp. 31–66
Plummer, K. (1983) *Documents of Life: an Introduction to the Problems and Literature of a Humanistic Method*, London: Allen and Unwin
Ruby, J. (ed.) (1989) *Visual Anthropology*, London: Harwood Academic
Scott, J. (1990) *A Matter of Record: Documentary Sources in Social Research*, Cambridge: Polity

On Multiple Methods, and Linking Methods

Brannen, J. (ed.) (1992) *Mixing Methods: Qualitative and Quantitative Research*, Aldershot: Avebury
Brewer, J. and Hunter, A. (1989) *Multimethod Research: a Synthesis of Styles*, London: Sage
Bryman, A. (1988) *Quantity and Quality in Social Research*, London: Unwin Hyman
Denzin, N.K. (1989) *The Research Act: a Theoretical Introduction to Sociological Methods*, 3rd edn, New Jersey: Prentice Hall (especially Chapter 10)
Fielding, N.G. and Fielding, J.L. (1986) *Linking Data*, London: Sage
Mason, J. (1994) 'Linking Qualitative and Quantitative Data Analysis' in A. Bryman and R.G. Burgess (eds) *Analyzing Qualitative Data*, London: Routledge

5

SAMPLING AND SELECTING

So far we have explored questions about research design, and examined three of the main methods used for generating qualitative data, but have said very little about how you decide whom you should interview, for example, or how many interviews you should conduct, or which or how many documents you should collect, or which and how many settings you should observe. Now we are going to move on to discuss these issues of sampling and selection.

In the broadest definition, sampling and selection are principles and procedures used to identify, choose, and gain access to relevant units which will be used for data generation by any method. These units will belong to or relate to a relevant wider population or universe. The principles and procedures can be governed by alternative underlying logics, although the term 'sampling' is very often associated solely with a logic derived from general laws of statistics and probability. This is unfortunate because in qualitative research the logic of probability is rarely employed, yet its strong association with the term 'sampling' means that alternative logics are less visibly practised and perhaps less well understood. Certainly, they are less well documented so that, with some notable exceptions, discussions of sampling are relatively absent from qualitative methods texts (examples of exceptions are Glaser and Strauss, 1967; Patton, 1987; Strauss and Corbin, 1990). However, qualitative research frequently does demand an alternative logic of sampling and selection, and in this chapter we will focus on difficult questions which researchers should ask themselves in order to establish what that logic should be and, as a consequence, with what principles and procedures their sampling and selection should be governed. One of the central aims of the chapter is to dispel any notion that somehow rigorous or systematic sampling strategies are not really important in qualitative research simply because it is often small scale or not amenable to the logic of mathematical probability. On the contrary, I want to suggest that sampling and selection – appropriately conceived and executed – are vitally important strategic elements of qualitative research.

THE LOGIC OF SAMPLING AND SELECTION IN QUALITATIVE RESEARCH

> Why should I sample? What is the purpose of sampling in my research?

The answer to this first question is likely to be fairly obvious, but it is nevertheless worth going through the motions of asking it so that you are clear about why *you* are sampling. It is usually considered necessary to sample or select because a complete census of the wider population or universe in which you are interested is either impossible, impractical to achieve, or simply not necessary. Actually, these reasons are usually combined so that, for example, if you wish to say something about British women's experiences of politics you may not feel it is necessary to interview *all* British women, but neither is it possible or practical to do so. Sometimes, however, you might wish to take a complete census of a specified universe or population. For example, you may wish to scrutinize all documents produced by a particular committee since its creation until the present day. Or you may wish to interview all female Members of Parliament in Britain. Such choices of course have already involved sampling decisions, in the sense that you have chosen the particular committee or the particular form of political organization that you are interested in, and the 'census' simply involves selecting every unit within these categories. For most purposes, then, you will wish to take a sample from a wider population rather than attempt to generate data from that population as a whole.

The other way to answer the question 'why sample?' or 'what is the purpose of sampling?' is to consider what work it is that you expect your sample to be able to do for you in your research. This is more complex, and requires that you work out in what way, and on what basis, data generated from your sample *signify* the wider population or universe in which you are interested. Much of the intellectual work involved in sampling and selecting concerns establishing an appropriate relationship between the sample or selection on the one hand, and the wider universe to which you see it as related on the other. And in order to achieve this, you will need to know the answer to the following questions.

> What is the wider universe or population from which I wish to sample? What is the nature of my interest in this universe or population?

There are potentially several answers to these questions in any research project. First, there are empirical answers which will concern, for example, the people, groups, countries, organizations, policies, discourses, social practices or activities in which you are interested. You are likely to end up with several empirical answers. So, for example, in a project concerning social welfare in contemporary Europe you might be interested in: the total adult population of Europe; the governments of all European Community member states; all European social security legislation since 1945; and all social security recipients in specified countries. These kinds of empirical answers to questions about your wider population or universe are, of course, already grounded within your broad ontological perspective. So, for example, the fact that you see the social world as meaningfully made up of people, political and geographical entities and boundaries, legal and administrative frameworks or whatever, is a statement of ontology, as we discussed in Chapter 2. These answers, then, are not somehow solely or neutrally empirical, and this should prompt you to reflect upon a second type of answer to the population or universe question: namely, answers which are directly and explicitly to do with social theory or social explanation. Here you need to think about the wider universe of social explanation in relation to which you have constructed your research questions. About which bodies of social explanation, or theoretical debate – for example, theories of the 'underclass', theories of welfare regimes, theories of gender relations, postmodernist understandings of power, theories of development, conceptions of the self – will you want to have something to say on the basis of your project? Your decisions about the nature of your interest in a wider universe or population will make some sampling choices more sensible and meaningful than others.

For example, if your project concerns gender and, in particular, your concern is with theories of gender *relations* (rather than say the *status* of women), then you will presumably be interested either in a literal population or universe of gender relations, or in a population which will enable you to speak of gender relations in a more interpretive sense. You are probably very unlikely to perceive the social world in terms of a large set of gender relations from which you can simply draw a smaller representative sample of gender relations. Similarly, you are unlikely to see gender relations as straightforwardly embodied in, or personified by, women and men, in a way which would make it meaningful simply to draw a representative sample of people by gender. However, you will have some sense of how a universe of gender relations might be constituted more theoretically, or interpretively (for example as *relations or interactions between* say, women and men; as *discourses which construct subjects* of gender relations; *as structures of power* within which women and men are differentially located; as gendered *genetic messages and codes*; as distinctive male and female *aptitudes and attributes*; and so on). If one or more of these are the constituent components or key defining features of the universe in which you have an interest, then they must form the building blocks for your sampling strategy. It is these features which you will want to represent or encapsulate somehow in your sample. Or, more interpretively, you will want to be able to say something theoretically about these features on the basis of data analyses derived from your sample. In other words, there is no point in drawing for interview a representative sample of all women and all men in Britain, if those total populations do not relate meaningfully to the universe – empirical or theoretical – in which you are interested.

> What should I sample? What are the
> relevant or 'sampleable' units?

Many researchers in the social sciences will, at some stage in their research, be sampling *people*, or conceptualizing people as their sampleable units. This is based on the notion that people are distinguishable, discrete and whole units or, in other words, we know what they are and we can tell them apart. The same might apply to other 'common sense' or 'real life' sampleable units such as documents or, less straightforwardly perhaps, discrete visual images (or sets of visual images, for example, films). To remain with the example of people for a moment, it is conventional in social research to classify people further for sampling and analytical purposes, for example on the basis of 'characteristics' like age, sex, class, ethnicity, occupation, specific life experiences. Often, these classifications are established as a gauge or scale for 'measuring' the representativeness of the sample of people against a wider population or universe of people (judged in terms of whether or not the sample displays these characteristics in similar proportions to the wider population). It is important to remember, therefore, that a representative sample constructed in this manner is representative only in terms of these known and specified characteristics of these known and specified sampleable units (that is, people). It is not necessarily representative in every possible sense (empirical or theoretical), but only in relation to the particular classification system used. Although this seems an obvious point, it is one which can be readily forgotten in the assumption that a 'representative' sample is representative of anything and everything in a wider population. These kinds of classification systems are of course also used in the construction of variables for data analysis, whereby the relationships between variables are explored. The term 'variable' in this sense refers to attributes on which relevant objects or sampleable units (in this case, people) differ.

It is important, however, to look behind and beyond these conventions, and to assess how relevant they are for your own particular project, and for qualitative research more generally. Specifically, you should ask yourself:

> Am I happy to use 'common sense' or
> 'real life' sampleable units, for
> example, people, documents?

Whilst people or discrete documents, and other 'common sense' or 'real life' units, might be appropriate units to sample, they equally might well not. In order to make a decision about this, you will need to think again about your intellectual puzzle, and what your research is really about. For example, if your ontological perspective tells you that people's *experiences* are meaningful, then you might want to think about sampling experiences, rather than people *per se*. In general, whether it be people, documents, visual images, settings for observation, or whatever, you may be more interested in *instances of what you see as relevant ontological properties of the social world* – for example, experiences - than in the 'common sense' or 'real life' units which seem most obviously apparent, such as people or places. In other words, you need to work out what is the most appropriate unit of classification to use in making sampling decisions, and common sense or everyday classifications may or may not suffice. Of course, sometimes you may end up using common sense classifications for pragmatic reasons, even though they are not ideal intellectually, but you must think through the implications of doing this.

> Am I happy to use the conventional or available classification systems of the units in question for sampling purposes?

If you decide, for intellectual or pragmatic reasons, to treat *people* as your sampleable units, for example, you will need to ask yourself whether the ways in which people are classified are relevant and useful to you in your sampling. So, for example, how useful and meaningful are conventional classifications which use 'characteristics' or 'attributes' such as age, gender, ethnicity, or social class? Your answer to this will depend first on how effectively you believe each of these classifying labels encapsulates a uniform and meaningful category of experience, or set of relevant instances; and secondly on how relevant these are to your research questions and your intellectual puzzle. In relation to the latter, you may simply decide that the conventional and available ways of classifying people are irrelevant for your purposes. In relation to the former, you may be happy to accept ethnicity, for example, as a uniform and meaningful category, or you may view it as too static, one-dimensional or cross-sectional an indicator of what are essentially complex and differentiated life experiences. This is not just a case of seeing ethnicity as more differentiated than the conventional divisions into well known ethnic groups would suggest; it also means that you may be taking issue with the way in which what you may see as complex and messy experiences, or understandings and meanings, or practices or biographies (or whatever are the relevant ontological properties), are reduced to a single static measure. In other words, you may be unwilling to accept that ethnicity, or indeed age or gender, can be treated as an attribute – or indeed as a variable – in such a straightforward way. Whatever your view, you *must* ask yourself what it is that you think these kinds of classifications represent, or what you see them as standing for. What does gender, or age, or ethnicity, or whatever, actually *mean* when it is used as a label in this way? (See Burgess, 1986, for a useful discussion of key variables in social investigation.)

> Am I happy to conceptualize characteristics, attributes, types, themes, experiences or instances as *variables*?

You may of course reject the idea of attributes or characteristics, and develop more sophisticated classifications based on, for example, the division of social existence into types, themes, experiences or instances. However, you will still need to begin to engage with the question of how far these can or should be conceptualized as variables for analytical purposes, since you may simply be creating a different set of variables rather than rejecting the notion of variable labels altogether. Although this is a question which relates more directly to your analytical than your sampling strategy, the two are in fact closely tied up together so that you cannot effectively sample without having some ideas about data analysis. We shall see later in this chapter, and in Chapter 7, that different sampling strategies support different approaches to analysis and explanation. Basically, if you are going to view characteristics, experiences, instances, or whatever, as variables, this implies a certain analytical logic as follows: variables are expressions of characteristics on which objects differ, and explanations are fashioned on the basis of an analysis of the connections and relationships (usually seen as causal) between variables (see Bryman and Cramer, 1990, for a discussion of the logic of variable analysis; see Blumer, 1956, for a classic critique of variable analysis; see also Pawson, 1989). This is anathema to many qualitative researchers partly because of the inadequacy of the labelling process whereby concepts are turned into variables, as already discussed, but also because of the superficial, circumstantial and one-dimensional nature of social explanation which they see it as producing.

When you can answer these questions, you will be getting close to the heart of your sampling strategy and logic. You may have decided what are your primary sampling units. However, you will need to view sampling in a more multidimensional way than I have so far encouraged you to do, and to think about the different dimensions along which your sampling units might be organized, and whether and how these dimensions intersect. Here are some of the key dimensions which may be relevant.

• Temporal dimensions. Whatever sampling units you choose, you will probably need to think about how these might be bounded by time. This means asking not just what you wish to sample, but when. You might be interested in experiences or practices or people at particular times (for example at coffee breaks, on holiday, in afternoon court sessions, in the 1940s), or experiences over a period of time (for example during a degree course, from the beginning to the end of compulsory schooling years, during membership of a particular 'subculture', during the American Civil War). You might also be interested in time itself as a focus for study. It is important to think about, and specify, your temporal parameters.

- Spatial or geographical dimensions. Again, whatever sampling units you choose, you should think about how and whether they are bounded by place, space and location. You might be interested in people, experiences, practices or whatever, in particular locations, for example at work, in class, in the pub, in Scandinavia, in the countryside. You might be interested primarily in the location itself, or movements between locations, or the ways in which space is used. Again, you will need to specify your parameters, and be clear about them.

- Organizational, administrative, social, cultural or linguistic dimensions. This requires you to think about how and whether your sampling units are located in relation to organizations, to administrative, social or cultural structures, to languages and so on. Are these dimensions relevant to your sampling units?

These dimensions can of course be conceptualized in a variety of ways, and you will need to work out exactly what you think they mean or stand for, just as you would with classifications of 'common sense' or 'real life' units and variables as discussed above. You will also need to think about how they intersect. So, for example, if you are planning a case study of an organization, you will need to work out not only which sampling units are relevant – first, which organization, then perhaps practices, policies, people, documents, within the organization – but also where the organization begins and ends (for the purposes of your study) in time and space. Is the organization spatially bounded, so that you will include only practices taking place 'behind the factory gates'? Are you interested in the experiences of staff when they are not in the workplace, as when they are off duty in terms of time, and at home in terms of space? Are you interested in the influence the organization might have on the local or national economy, or on its interface with health and safety legislation, and so on?

I have posed a difficult range of questions about what you might sample. Questions like these are very closely tied up with the issue of *validity* which was introduced in Chapter 2 (and which is discussed further in Chapter 7). In its most general terms, a judgement about whether data analysis is valid is a judgement about whether or not it measures, explicates or illuminates whatever it claims to measure, explicate or illuminate. So, for example, in judging the validity of an analysis of religious belief one might ask does this study actually tell us about *religious* belief as opposed to some other kind of belief, or does it actually tell us about belief rather than religious *behaviour*, and so on? Or, can the author of an analysis of cultural change demonstrate convincingly that they are tapping into *culture* – however they define it – rather than, say, unconnected sets of individual behaviours? Does a study of personality development convincingly illuminate the development of *personalities*, rather than, say, behaviours, or even cultures? In other words, does the analysis really get at the kinds of issues and concepts it claims to get at? A major part of the answer to this question will depend upon how effectively the researcher has thought about what they should sample, or what are the sampleable units in their study. This is because, to pursue the religious beliefs example, being able to produce a valid analysis of religious belief is dependent upon successfully accessing the conduits or vessels within which such beliefs are contained, be these people's minds, people's actions, people's words, religious discourses, and so on. For each sampling decision, therefore, you should ask whether this person, or these people, or this or these documents, or this or these instances or experiences, can potentially tell you what you want to know. Finding a successful answer to the question of what you should sample contributes to the ultimate production of analytical validity by ensuring that you are looking in the right places when you go about the process of data generation.

Of course deciding what to sample also involves questions about *reliability* (see Chapters 2 and 7), since you will need to be making assessments about how accurate, reliable or authentic a set of data can be generated from those particular sources, be they people, documents, organizations, or whatever.

Having addressed questions about what you wish to sample, and from what wider universe or population you wish your sample to be drawn, you must confront the key question, the answer to which – when taken together with the answers you have already arrived at – will determine your sampling strategy. This is:

> What relationship do I want to establish, or do I assume exists, between the sample or selection I am making, and a wider population or universe?

This question takes us right to the heart of the logic of sampling strategy, and it is very important that qualitative researchers grapple – and grapple successfully – with it because, as I suggested at the beginning of the chapter, they may wish to depart from 'conventional' sampling logic. The first point to grasp in relation to this question is that there are a number of possible answers. In other words, it is possible to conceive of different types of relationship between your sample and a wider population or universe. Let us consider some of the most significant examples of these relationships, beginning with the one which most commonly characterizes conventional, probability sampling.

- A relationship where the sample is *representative* of a wider population or universe. This usually involves trying to select a sample which is representative of the total empirical population which you wish to study, in the sense that the sample displays characteristics (like age, gender, ethnicity, class in a population of people) in similar proportions and patterns to the total population about which you wish to make generalizations. This requires, of course, that the parameters of the total population are known, as are some of the population's key characteristics, and these pieces of information constitute a sampling frame from which your sample can be drawn. In this type of sampling, the aim is to achieve a representative microcosm of the population which the researcher wishes to study, so that they can claim that patterns discovered within the microcosm are likely to appear in similar shapes and proportions in that total population, whatever it may be. Statistical conventions are used to calculate the probability that patterns observed in the sample will exist in the wider population.

  This is probably the most commonly understood form of sampling logic, yet it is also probably the least commonly used logic in qualitative research, for a number of reasons. Perhaps most importantly, much qualitative research uses a different analytical logic, and one which is not particularly well supported by the generation of a representative sample. This is outlined below and in Chapter 7. This means that representative sampling may not be the most effective and efficient way either to generate data which will address the research questions of the study, or to develop analysis and theory. Furthermore, the pursuit of representativeness often requires the construction of very large samples which make the use of qualitative data generation methods very time consuming and costly (and in many instances therefore impossible to achieve). The patterns observed in data generated from a representative sample may therefore necessarily be rather superficial, and this approach does not readily facilitate the detailed exploration of social processes. For many qualitative researchers the consequently limited gains of having a representative sample are not offset by the substantial losses in terms of sampling and analytical sensitivity. Finally, the parameters of a total population and its key characteristics are not always known quantities, or are not adequately 'measured' by characteristics which are known. For example, as we have seen, commonly defined 'variables' such as age or gender may be of limited relevance in your conceptualization of what is the total population. More likely, they will be too static or cross-sectional and not sufficiently processual or conceptually rich. In other

words, you may decide that known characteristics of an empirical
population do not represent meaningful, coherent or consistent categorizations because they are too flat, static, one-dimensional or simplistic.

The consequences of all of these factors are therefore that, first, you
may decide that the pursuit of representativeness in a sample is not the
most suitable way to make theoretical and analytical advances in relation
to your research questions; secondly, you may find the criteria for
judging or measuring the representativeness of a sample to be flawed or
superficial; thirdly, it may therefore not actually be possible to judge the
representativeness of the sample against the population in question; and
fourthly, it may therefore be impossible to devise methods for drawing a
sample which might be considered representative in the first place.

- A relationship between sample and the wider universe which is *ad hoc or
  unspecifiable* in any way. This is undesirable, since it severely limits the
  analytical potential of the study. It is nevertheless included in the list,
  because it is sometimes, erroneously, seen as the only alternative where
  a representative relationship between sample and wider universe is
  impossible, or when the precise parameters of the wider universe are
  unknown. However, whilst it is often not possible to calculate the degree
  to which a sample represents its wider universe, this does not mean that
  qualitative researchers should or can simply construct a sample in an
  entirely *ad hoc* way.

- A relationship where the sample is designed to provide a close-up,
  detailed or *meticulous view of particular units*, which may constitute
  processes, types, categories, cases or examples which are relevant to or
  appear within the wider universe. You may indeed select just one unit for
  detailed scrutiny, such as an organization, a geographical or spatial
  location, a language, a person, a lifetime, a document, a social
  experience, a set of relationships, a conversation, a dream. The purpose
  of selecting one or more units may be that, for example, you wish to
  demonstrate in a detailed and rounded way the operations of a particular
  set of social processes in a specified context (rather than, for example,
  examine surface patterns within a sample which can – because the sample
  is a representative one – be generalized to a wider population).
  However, you will still need to be clear about the principles which you
  use to select the processes, types, categories, cases or examples, and to
  be able to specify what their relevance is in relation to the wider universe.
  We will consider what such principles might be shortly.

- A relationship where the sample is designed to encapsulate a *relevant
  range* of units in relation to the wider universe, but not to represent it
  directly. The range referred to here might incorporate a range of
  experiences, characteristics, processes, types, categories, cases or
  examples, and so on. You should have a strategic purpose in selecting
  your specified relevant range which means that the relationship between

your sample and the wider universe is not *ad hoc*. Again though, you will need to be clear about exactly what kind of relationship you are establishing.

These last two examples, then, leave open the question of what kind of relationship exists between sample and wider population. Both examples suggest that the relationship will not be one of straightforward representation, although of course you may wish to include units in your sample which you know commonly to occur in the wider universe, or which are at least not untypical of units occurring in the wider universe. But there are other possibilities too.

You may, for example, decide that certain units have a special or pivotal significance in relation to your research questions and your intellectual puzzle. This *may* be because they commonly occur in the wider universe (and in that sense you are defining them as empirically significant), but it is more likely that you will be defining their significance theoretically. This may involve selecting units which occur infrequently rather than commonly in the wider universe. There are many ways of conceptualizing significance theoretically, some of which are outlined in the discussion of analysis in Chapter 7, but at a general level in relation to sampling it means that you will wish to select units which *will enable you to make key comparisons and to test and develop theoretical propositions*. This links sampling very directly into the process of generating theory and explanation 'inductively' from or through data. This implies that, when you determine your sampling strategy, you will be thinking ahead to the kind of analysis which you are likely to conduct. It also suggests that you will be doing something more than simply aggregating data gained from all your sampling units and noting frequencies of patterns and distributions. Furthermore, it means that qualitative researchers should ensure that there is a very direct link between their sampling strategy, their data analysis and the type of social explanation they intend to construct. Making such a link will influence your sampling strategy both conceptually (that is, what is its logic) and procedurally (that is, how it is executed).

We will discuss the practice of sampling and selection shortly, but in terms of the logic of your sampling strategy, if you are constructing a non-representative sample with the aim of making key comparisons and testing and developing theoretical propositions, then what you are likely to be doing is some form of *theoretical sampling* or *purposive sampling*. This contrasts with statistical or probability sampling, which is that used to generate empirically representative samples. Probably the most well known version of this kind of theoretical sampling strategy is that developed in Glaser and Strauss's classic *The Discovery of Grounded Theory* (Glaser and Strauss, 1967), but many qualitative researchers will use a version of theoretical or purposive sampling without necessarily following the precise techniques and strategies advocated by Glaser and Strauss, and later in more detail by Strauss (Strauss, 1987). In its more general form, theoretical sampling means selecting groups or categories to study on the basis of their relevance to your research questions, your theoretical position and analytical framework, your analytical practice, and most importantly the explanation or account which you are developing. Theoretical sampling is concerned with constructing a sample (sometimes called a study group) which is meaningful theoretically, because it builds in certain characteristics or criteria which help to develop and test your theory and explanation.

However, you must ensure that you do not simply pick those sampling units which will support your argument and disregard those inconvenient ones which do not. You can and should make sure that you sample in a way which will help you not only to develop your theory or explanation, but also to test it, and you need to build in a mechanism for doing this. A classic way to do this, derived from procedures of 'analytic induction' (see Denzin, 1989, Chapter 7), is to seek out negative instances or contradictory cases in relation to your developing analytical ideas. In other words, you should use your sampling strategy not simply to acquire units from which you will generate data which support your analysis or explanation, but also to show that you have rigorously looked for cases or instances which do not fit with your ideas or which cannot be accounted for by the explanation which you are developing. If you cannot find any, and if you can show that you have looked in places where such negative cases are likely to occur, then your explanation is strengthened. If you can find some, then you will need to modify your explanation. So, for example, if your theory suggests that a certain constellation of experiences in people's lives is likely to encourage them to be politically active, then you could search for someone who is politically active but does not have that set of experiences; or you could search for someone with that set of experiences who is not politically active. Then the analytical task is to understand the differences and to adapt your theory accordingly. Another version involves selecting the most unlikely scenario in which a given process is 'hypothesized' to occur (this being established on the basis of existing research and theory, or upon the analysis you have developed of your own data so far). If the process does occur, even in that setting, then the claim you wish to make about it may be strengthened.

The search for negative instances in the analytical process is discussed more fully in Chapter 7, but the point in relation to sampling is that it can and should be driven by the analytical and explanatory logic you propose to adopt. In particular, your capacity to make *generalizations* on the basis of your analysis, and the way in which you will be able to do this, will be crucially influenced by the strategy you have adopted for sampling (see Platt, 1988, for a useful discussion of links between sampling and generalization).

It is worth reiterating at this point that representative sampling comes with statistical conventions which can be used to substantiate or measure the relationship between sample and wider universe and, in particular, to judge how well one represents the other. Although I have also suggested that qualitative researchers may find such conventions unsatisfactory in some instances, it is important to note that the conventions exist and are widely recognized. However, given that theoretical and purposive sampling are not based on a notion of empirical representativeness, the issue of how one substantiates the relationship between the sample and the wider universe is not so clear cut, and it is, therefore, even more important for researchers to specify exactly what they see this relationship to be. Theoretical or purposive sampling can be criticized for being *ad hoc* and vague if not employed systematically. It is very important to have a sampling *strategy* in your research, and to be able to explain its logic. If you do not do this, you run the risk that your sampling will be misunderstood, and judged by statistical criteria (that is, as though you were trying to produce a sample statistically representative of a wider population). It is therefore vital to keep a record of the sampling decisions you take, and the basis on which you take them, so that you can spell out (in your theses, publications and so on) exactly what you did and why. You do not have to engage in statistical sampling to be able to demonstrate that you have proceeded in a logical and systematic way, and indeed a failed attempt to justify what you have done in quasi-statistical terms is likely only to reduce the strength with which you are able to make claims about the rigour of your alternative sampling procedures. But you do have to be able to construct an alternative – and convincing – logic.

THE PRACTICE OF SAMPLING AND SELECTING

Not all qualitative sampling fits the theoretical sampling mould precisely, but there is nearly always a concern with sampling in an analytical or theoretical way (rather than an empirical or statistical way). Once you have worked out what overall logic is going to guide your sampling decisions, you will be in a position to start thinking in more practical or grounded terms about what those decisions are going to be, that is: how many units to sample, when to draw your sample, and so on. Let us begin with the questions which most vex many qualitative researchers.

> How many units should I sample?
> How large should my sample be?

The answer to these questions is not likely to be straightforward. If you are using a theoretical or purposive sampling strategy, then whether or not the sample is big enough to be statistically representative of a total population is not your major concern. However, you will wish to include particular units, or a range of units, from which you can generate data which will help you to develop your theory, and that range *may* end up being quite large. So, it is possible to end up sampling reasonably large numbers, but you arrive at that result for a different reason, and by a different logic, than you would with statistical forms of sampling. Qualitative samples are usually small for practical reasons to do with the costs, especially in terms of time and money, of generating and analysing qualitative data, but in my view there is no inherent reason why a qualitative sample *must be* small.

The logic of theoretical or purposive sampling is that you select units which will enable you to make meaningful comparisons in relation to your research questions, your theory and the type of explanation you wish to develop (see Chapter 7 for a further discussion). This means you must think about:

> What do I wish to compare?

When you are making comparisons you are unlikely to be attempting to compare sampling unit with sampling unit as though they are representative of all such units. Similarly, you are unlikely to see the sampling units as straightforwardly comparable in and of themselves because, as discussed earlier, you may have selected them because they provide *access* in an interpretive sense to something that you are interested in, rather than actually *being* what you are interested in. Therefore, the units which you will use to make comparisons in your analysis may not be an exact reflection of the units you have used for sampling. You may, for example, have sampled people, but wish to make comparisons of experiences. The people involved may have had uneven numbers and types of the kinds of experiences you wish to compare so, for some purposes, you may compare the people, and for others you may compare specific types of experience. You may wish to make comparisons of complex sets of experiences, or experiential processes, which are not readily encapsulated in the idea of a 'characteristic' of a person, which can be used as a variable to classify that person for purposes of comparison with other people and variables.

> Why do I wish to make comparisons?
> How – according to what logic –
> does comparison help me to develop
> social explanation?

As discussed, qualitative methods are usually used when the object of study is some form of social process or meaning or experience which needs to be understood and explained in a rounded way, rather than by attempting to understand, for example, causal patterns by analysing connections between static or snapshot variables. Bertaux and Bertaux-Wiame (1981) claim that the size of sample is dictated by the social process under scrutiny. According to Bertaux and Bertaux-Wiame, you sample until you reach theory-saturation point, that is until you know that you have a picture of what is going on and can generate an appropriate explanation for it. This point is reached when your data begin to stop telling you anything new about the social process under scrutiny. Bertaux and Bertaux-Wiame have been criticized for this view on the basis that it is rather *ad hoc* and unsystematic (it raises the question of how the researcher can demonstrate that saturation point really was reached), but the principle that your sample size should help you to *understand the process*, rather than to represent (statistically) a population, is a good one.

Deciding how large your sample should be therefore involves asking why you wish to make comparisons, which in turn should encourage you to reflect upon the logic through which you intend to develop and test social explanations. The basic principle is likely to be something like: 'instead of establishing causality, for example, on the basis of connections and relationships between variables such as age and voting behaviour, I am attempting to develop explanations (whether or not these are causal) through detailed scrutiny of how processes work in particular contexts.' You cannot, however, expect a context to be representative of all contexts of that type, unless you have sampled in a way which ensures this.

This principle of understanding the process rather than representing a population must be kept clearly in view when you are deciding how many units of a particular type you will select in order to constitute, for example, a relevant range for purposes of comparison and explanation. Do not fall into the trap of supposing that, because you select one unit of a particular type, this can somehow represent *all* units of this type. So, for example, if you decide that a relevant range of units might be people of different ages selected for interview, and so you select ten people, each of whose ages fall within a specified five year period, you must not let yourself slide back into a statistical or probability logic whereby you expect the one 55 year old in your study to be representative of all 55 year olds. Instead, you must remember that the units which you have chosen to constitute a range are intended to allow you to generate data to explore processes, similarities and differences, to test and develop theory and explanation to account for those similarities and differences, rather than to make statistical comparisons between the units themselves within the range, and to infer causality on that basis. In other words, you are expecting the interview with your 55 year old to provide access to qualitative data which will help you to make sense of, for example, voting behaviour and its location and development within the life experience, biography, and so on, of that person. You are emphatically *not* expecting your 55 year old to be a representative for other 55 year olds simply because they possess the 'characteristic' of being 55.

> What are the key comparisons for my
> study? What would 'negative
> instances' look like?

The answers to these questions must be driven by your research questions and your intellectual puzzle, but also are likely to be influenced by the ideas and theories you develop in the process of generating and analysing data. Thus, at the beginning of your research, you will have some ideas about key comparisons based on, for example, existing research and theory. These will help you to decide not only how your sample should be constituted, but how large it will need to be, so that such comparisons can feasibly be made. You may also begin your research with ideas about what 'negative instances' would look like, but these are likely to develop more fully as you begin to fashion your own explanation of the phenomena under scrutiny.

Taken together, all of these factors suggest that the answer to the question of how large your sample should be is that it should be large enough to make meaningful comparisons. In other words, there is not a fixed answer, because it depends upon what a meaningful set of comparisons would look like in relation to your specific research project, its research questions and intellectual puzzle, and the kind of social explanation you are striving to produce. Your guiding practice should be to be explicit about why particular comparisons might be meaningful, bearing in mind your answers to the earlier questions about what you are sampling and why. You will need, therefore, to keep asking yourself: why is this or that unit or group relevant? In what ways would including it or them in my study help me in developing the overall kind of explanation I wish to develop, or in understanding the process I wish to understand? This is the logic which should drive your decisions about which units to include, as well as how many units to include.

You will need to develop a practical and systematic method for making and recording your decisions about sample size. Whilst determining your final sample size is a matter of intellectual judgement based on the logic of making meaningful comparisons, developing and testing your explanations, I do not recommend that you rely solely on your intellectual intuition to 'know' when you have sampled enough. Instead, many qualitative researchers use a system of quotas, targets or grids, both to set out initially what their intentions are in relation to sampling units and numbers, and subsequently to keep track of how far their sampling practice is fulfilling these intentions, and how far it needs to be modified – for example by a search for negative instances – in the light of their developing analysis. Thus, in recommending that you specify some initial targets, I am not suggesting that you should see these as entirely rigid and unchangeable.

You might, for example, construct lists, tables or grids, which document your initial quotas and targets. Remember that a sampling unit may or may not be equivalent to a 'common sense' or 'real life' unit such as a person or a discrete document. You may wish to sample experiences or instances, the numbers of which may not precisely correspond with the numbers of 'common sense' or 'real life' units like people or documents which you ultimately include: one person may, for example, have several of the experiences you are interested in, or one document may contain more than one instance. Your list, table or grid should specify roughly the range and number of different sampling units you want to include, and also give some ideas about how these might cross-cut each other. So, for example, are you happy to include people who have multiple experiences of the kind you are interested in, or do you require each experience to be embodied in a different person? Does it matter what constellations of experiences people have – do you want some people to have specific combinations of experience? Would it be alright if all the people in your study who had one particularly interesting experience were also all of the same age? Or do you want particular experiences to be more widely distributed across age ranges? The answers to these questions clearly depend on how and why you are going to want to make comparisons. Figure 5.1 provides a simple example of how you might set out such a list or chart of quota targets, based on a section of the quota list devised for a real project on the topic of 'Migration, Kinship and Household Change'.[1] Note that the number of total experiences targeted exceeds the total number of interviewees, suggesting that some interviewees will have more than one experience. Some combinations of experience are specified, others are left open. There is also some flexibility in the gender quotas, whereby the gender of 10 target interviewees is left unspecified.

The purpose of preparing a list, chart or grid of this type is to make sure that you are thinking systematically about the kinds of sampling units you want to include in your study, and their numbers. So, for example, if your

Figure 5.1 *Example of a quota target list*

Total sample size = 60 interviewees
To include:

- at least 30 people with experience of *divorce and/or remarriage*
- at least 20 people over the age of 65 who either already have some *personal care needs*, or can anticipate needing some help in the foreseeable future
- at least 20 people who have experience (past, present or anticipated future) of being actual or potential *carers* for elderly relatives
- at least 25 people who have made a *residential move* related in some way to divorce, remarriage or elderly care
- at least 15 people who have *not moved* house in these kinds of circumstances
- at least 25 *women*, ensuring that there are at least 3 in each of the above categories
- At least 25 *men*, ensuring that there are at least 3 in each of the above categories

strategy is to include a 'relevant range' of units in your sample, the discipline of producing this kind of chart will ensure that you do not simply collect an '*ad hoc* or idiosyncratic range'. However, as stated earlier, you should not necessarily view your initial targets and quotas as entirely rigid and binding, since you will want to incorporate some ongoing flexibility to allow your sampling strategy to be sensitive to the realities of data generation, and the discoveries made during data analysis. You may not fully know, when you begin to sample, what constitutes a relevant range. You should therefore engage with the following question.

> # When should I make my sampling decisions?

Theoretical or purposive sampling is a set of procedures where the researcher manipulates their analysis, theory, and sampling activities *interactively* during the research process, to a much greater extent than in statistical sampling. This sampling strategy is broadly intended to facilitate a process whereby researchers generate and test theory from the analysis of their data (sometimes called inductive reasoning), rather than using data to test out or falsify a pre-existing theory (sometimes called deductive reasoning). In this latter model, sampling decisions are generally taken prior to the generation and subsequent analysis of data, which are seen as independent stages in the research process. With theoretical or purposive sampling, although you are likely to want to make some early decisions about sampling as we have seen, you are also likely to want to review these at certain stages.

Therefore, in theoretical or purposive sampling, the processes of sampling, data generation and data analysis are viewed more interactively. This means that a qualitative researcher must work out not only when to start making sampling decisions, but also when to stop. You need to be able to make informed decisions about sampling – that is, decisions which are informed by analysis, theory and explanation. Looking for negative instances is one example of that. Your theoretical position at the beginning of your research will come out of your reading of existing research, other literature, and possibly some preliminary research or observation of your own. But as you go on your theory and developing explanation themselves will be informed by your analysis of your own data. If your sampling strategy is to be informed by theory, and in turn help to develop your theory and explanation, this implies that you do not have to decide upon it once and for all at the beginning, because at that point in your research you may not be in the best position to make such precise decisions. Instead, you may wish to make some preliminary decisions about sampling which will lead you into a position where you can make informed decisions subsequently (some form of pilot study is an initial way of doing this). Therefore, the process is one involving the setting of some initial sampling quotas and targets, and their subsequent systematic review.

If you do decide to postpone some sampling decisions, or to set tentative targets which may be revised, you must be systematic about those subsequent decisions. You should build into your research practice mechanisms which are designed to help you to review your sampling strategy at relevant times, and make informed decisions about how to proceed. You may wish to set specific dates or points in the research process when you do this. The use of targets, quotas and grids as outlined above will help you to be systematic in this way, because they can act as a baseline against which to measure both how well your sampling strategy is filling your quotas, and also how useful those quotas continue to be (see Finch and Mason, 1990). The consequence of this kind of 'stocktaking' exercise may be that you want to modify your quotas, or introduce new quotas. For example, as you begin to formulate an explanation of, say, gender relations in the rock music industry, you may discover that particular life experiences which you had not previously thought of now seem to be important influences on the career trajectories of male and female rock musicians, or that the activities of a particular record company seem influential. You may want to adjust your sampling quotas at this stage to include these, and if you have set clear and strategic targets, and kept good records of how well these have been met, you will quickly and easily be able to estimate the implications of making this kind of change at this particular point in your research. Similarly, you may find that you have practical difficulties in filling your quota targets satisfactorily, which necessitate some change of plan. Again, you will be able to do this in a strategic fashion if you have adopted some kind of systematic mechanism for making and recording sampling decisions.

It can be a great help to talk to your supervisor or colleagues about your sampling progress, and about any potential decisions you want to make. Getting a second opinion can help you work things through, and the discipline of having to explain your strategy to others will help you to make explicit the multitude of sometimes half-formed ideas you are operating with. Keep a record of the whole process, and the basis on which you make decisions, so that you can justify your strategy afterwards. This is not just so that you can defend your research to other people: keeping a record of what you decided and why is a good way to start developing your own principles for analysis of the data set as a whole.

> How, or by what methods and techniques, can I best achieve the kind of sample I want?

You will need to pick a method of sample selection which is both practicable and allows you to establish an appropriate relationship between your sample and the wider universe, incorporate appropriate numbers of specific sampling units and so on. This can be quite difficult, and you will need to try to identify a suitable 'sampling frame'. A sampling frame is a resource from which you can select your smaller sample. It will help you in filling quota targets if the sampling frame contains some information about the sampling units which is relevant to those quotas. Whatever frame you choose, your sampling practice will thenceforward be influenced by the parameters of that frame. Let us consider an example. You may perhaps choose electoral registers as a frame for sampling people. In Britain, electoral registers currently contain names and addresses of household residents who are aged over 18 and who are registered electors. The information is organized by household, and by residential address. You can use such information to make your selections, or to gain further information to help you to make selections. You might gain further information by, for example, contacting people or households directly, or you might make some visual assessment of the household and its location, or you might do some cross-referencing with other potential sampling frames – for example, the telephone directory. The question of how you make decisions about which sampling units to select from your sampling frame of course depends on the logic of your sampling strategy and, in particular, the relationship you are trying to establish between your sample and your wider population. If you want a sample which is statistically representative of all registered electors, then you are likely to use a random method of selection, or a stratified random method whereby you make random selections within certain categories (for example, geographical location of household). If you wish to target men only, then you may be influenced by the names of electors in your choices, although of course sex cannot always be read straightforwardly from given names.

There are at least three difficulties which are commonly encountered in relation to identifying and using sampling frames:

- Although a sampling frame is available, it does not provide enough relevant information about the potential sampling units to enable you to make considered selections. So, for example, as well as knowing that people are registered electors, knowing their names, and where they live, you may want to know about their experience of foreign travel, or their educational qualifications, or their sexuality. Whilst you might have a sampling frame such as the electoral register which tells you something about people, it is unlikely to give you access to the full range of factors and experiences which you are interested in. Furthermore, the frame may be partial in its coverage. The British electoral register, for example, will not give you names and addresses of all people who are potentially eligible to vote. Homeless people are excluded, as are people who are not officially registered as electors. Similarly, the register may provide inaccurate information, for example where members of a household have moved since the compilation of the register.

In these cases either you can try to find an alternative or supplementary sampling frame, or you can try to devise a two-stage method – for example a superficial survey of selected registered electors – for generating the information which you require, and effectively therefore for producing your own sampling frame from which to make subsequent selections. Similarly, with documentary research, you might make some kind of preliminary assessment of a set of documents and, on that basis, produce a sampling frame for further selections. These kinds of procedures can, however, be rather consuming of resources and unwieldy, so you will need to think carefully about how feasible they are.

- A sampling frame is available, but the defining characteristics of the frame are specific in ways which are not helpful to your research. So, to use one of the examples cited above, if you are interested in people's experiences of foreign travel you might try to gain access to the database of a travel agent. However, that database may be specific in ways not helpful to your research, for example it may contain clients who live in one particular geographical area, or who are mostly of only one or two socio-economic classes, or who mostly visit only a small range of destinations or engage in particular types of travel, and so on. If you are hoping to produce a sample of travellers representative of all travellers by, for example, making random selections from your sampling frame, then the biased nature of this frame is clearly a problem. But even if this is not your intention, the shape and nature of the sampling frame will of course influence the kinds of selections you are able to make. The general message here is that you must think carefully and critically about the parameters and specificity of any sampling frame which you use.

- A sampling frame is not available. This is a very common problem in social research. Very often there is simply not in existence an appropriate resource from which you can sample. This means that you will have to think about whether you can generate your own sampling frame, or whether you can draw on a number of partially adequate frames to piece together your sample. You might, alternatively, use a method like 'snowball' sampling, whereby you begin with one sampling unit – usually a person – and ask them to put you in touch with others of a similar or known type. In a sense, this will also produce a sampling frame for you, and you should ask yourself the same questions about how adequate it is. Does it matter that the units – people – might know each other? Does it matter that decisions about who should be included in your sample are, at least in part, in the hands of the initial contacts whose help you seek in gaining further contacts?

These issues, and how you resolve them, are clearly influenced by intellectual considerations, but also by the practicalities of actually getting your sampling done. Indeed, practical considerations can seem quite overwhelming in the process of sampling, and I probably therefore do not have to remind you to ask yourself the following question:

> Is my sampling strategy practical and feasible?

Your sampling practice will be influenced by all kinds of practical considerations and, whilst these should not drive the intellectual decisions you take, they must of course inform those decisions. Again, the importance of having a sampling strategy should be emphasized here so that, faced with practical difficulties and constraints, you are able to take strategic decisions, and to have a broader understanding of their consequences for your study. The kinds of practical matters you should ask yourself about include:

> Can I gain access to the kind of sample I require? How long will all this take?

You must ask yourself realistically whether you will be able to fill your quota targets using your chosen sampling logic and methods. There is little point in inventing a highly sophisticated and detailed set of quotas if you have no practical method for filling these. Given the importance of strategy and quotas in qualitative sampling, however, the onus is upon you to find practical methods, rather than to abandon strategic planning. However, you must ask yourself how long this is likely to take, and what kind of commitment of other resources you are likely to have to make. If, for example, you will need to conduct a preliminary scan of 5,000 documents in order to devise a means for selecting 500, you should try to work out how long that first stage will take. You may need to think quite carefully about how many documents you will have to subject to the initial scan in order to produce a frame large enough to select the sample size you require. Do you have enough time to do this? What are the other options?

Once you have identified your sampling units, how certain are you that access to them will be forthcoming? If, for example, your units are people, you must bear in mind that some people will be willing to participate and some will not. 'Access' is difficult to define, as we have seen. You may be given permission to do the research by, for example, a manager in an organization, but does that (or should that?) guarantee you access to the employees, to the clients or customers, to the filing system, and so on. You may need to negotiate with gatekeepers, or ethical committees, which again will drain your time and resources. You will not always know at the beginning of the research whether or not your application for access will be successful. You will therefore need contingency plans, or at least some ideas about what you will do if you cannot draw a sample, and gain access to it, in the way you propose.

> How many interviews, observations, diaries, documents, visits to archives, visits to the cinema, study trips abroad, and so on can I carry out given the available resources?

In answering this question you have to bear in mind the handling, organization, and analysis of the data, as well as their generation. For example, doing 20 qualitative interviews at two hours apiece may not seem to take very long in the grand scale of things, but if you are going to transcribe them, and search the transcripts for themes and categories, and develop case studies, and so on, you will begin to realize that the commitment of resources is quite large. The same even goes for making 20 trips to the cinema if you are doing this in anything more than a recreational way.

> Is my sampling strategy ethical?

You may have very good intellectual reasons for wishing to make certain sampling selections, and they may be practicable, but you nevertheless feel that such selections would be unethical. For example, a sampling frame for a study of inheritance might be the death notices in a local newspaper. However, you are unlikely to feel that it is acceptable to approach recently bereaved people using this method. Or, you may have unofficial access to private documents which would be very useful for your study. Or, you may be able to identify people whom you would like to include in your study, but you may suspect that such inclusion would place them in a difficult or dangerous position. The point really is that decisions about sampling cannot be divorced from the wider ethics of your research practice.

CONCLUSION

The conventions for sampling in qualitative research are less clear cut or well established than for statistical sampling and quantitative research. I do not think it is possible, however, to provide a recipe which sets out how sampling should be done in every qualitative research project, or even a set of common principles. Instead, I have focused on a core set of difficult questions with which you should engage in order to come to sensible, strategic and grounded sampling decisions for qualitative research. Different types of project, of research puzzle, and of data generation method will raise different sampling issues and problems, and although I have not been able to cover these in detail, I have tried to give a flavour of some of them in this chapter.

A recurrent theme throughout the chapter has concerned the link which can and should be established between sampling strategies, the process of data analysis, and the construction of explanations. It is to questions about how you might sort, organize, and analyse your qualitative data that we shall turn in the following two chapters.

NOTE

1   Figure 5.1 shows a small section of a longer quota target list designed for this project. The project was funded by the Economic and Social Research Council between 1994 and 1996, under the direction of Dr R. Flowerdew, Prof. R. Davies (both of Lancaster University) and Dr J. Mason (Leeds University), grant no. L315253007.

FURTHER READING

Bryman, A. and Cramer, D. (1990) *Quantitative Analysis for Social Scientists*, London: Routledge (Chapter 6 'Sampling and Statistical Significance' gives a good introduction to the logic of statistical sampling)

Burgess, R.G. (ed.) (1986) *Key Variables in Social Investigation*, London: Routledge

Finch, J. and Mason, J. (1990) 'Decision Taking in the Fieldwork Process: Theoretical Sampling and Collaborative Working' in R.G. Burgess (ed.) *Studies in Qualitative Methodology*, vol. 2, JAI Press, pp. 25–50

Glaser, B.G. and Strauss, A.L. (1967) *The Discovery of Grounded Theory*, Chicago: Aldine (especially the chapter on 'Theoretical Sampling')

Platt, J. (1988) 'What Can Case Studies Do?' in R.G. Burgess (ed.) *Studies in Qualitative Methodology*, vol. 1, JAI Press, pp. 1–23 (provides an excellent discussion of the ways in which sampling and data analysis can be linked in case study research)

Strauss, A. and Corbin, J. (1990) *Basics of Qualitative Research: Grounded Theory Procedures and Techniques*, London: Sage (Chapter 11 'Theoretical Sampling')

6

SORTING, ORGANIZING AND INDEXING QUALITATIVE DATA

The key question for this chapter and the next involves how to construct and present a convincing explanation or argument on the basis of qualitative data. This is of course a question which troubles many a would-be qualitative researcher who can see the merits of a qualitative approach to data generation, but is less clear about what can be done with the 'products'. 'Doing something with the products' covers a potentially wide range of activities, from the routine organization and handling of data, to working out whether it is possible to make generalizations to some wider reality or universe. This chapter will deal with the former, and Chapter 7 with the latter. Both will pose difficult questions which, amongst other things, demonstrate that the elements within this range are interconnected and therefore that one's approach to analysis of all kinds – including sorting data and building explanations – should be both strategic and internally consistent.

In this chapter I am going to outline three broad approaches to the task of sorting and organizing qualitative data. They are: cross-sectional and categorical indexing; non-cross-sectional data organization; and the use of diagrams and charts. These three are not, however, mutually exclusive alternatives and in practice you are likely to want to use elements of all three. They are differentiated to some extent, however, both technically and epistemologically, because they involve different techniques and activities, and also because they support different modes of social explanation. Before you can decide which approaches you wish to use, however, you will need to know how to recognize and 'read' your data.

RECOGNIZING AND 'READING' DATA

The impulse to impose some form of organization and order on your data can seem overwhelming when you are faced with a mass of apparently unconnected notes and scribblings, interview tapes, transcribed conversations, documents, photographs, maps, diagrams, hunches and ideas, and so on. At the very least, you are likely to want to organize your material physically into different boxes or filing cabinets, or computer files or directories, according to some form of cross-sectional indexing and cataloguing system. In other words, you will want to use a system which is consistent across the whole data set (or large parts of it), or consistent within each of your data sets if you have more than one. You will want to number, name or otherwise identify the boxes as well as the individual texts, documents, videos, artefacts, or whatever. You may wish to file fieldnotes chronologically, or thematically, or both, so that you will know how to retrieve them and be able to do so quickly and with the minimum of fuss. You will probably want to cross-reference different types of data with each other, for example, interview transcripts with fieldnotes, photographs, specific documents, and so on. Again, you will need to devise a system for doing this – for example, should the cross-referencing be chronological or thematic? What makes sense in terms of the types of connections you are wishing to make? You will need to ensure that your records are confidential and are kept carefully, securely and responsibly, and in accordance with data protection and privacy legislation.

At first sight, this kind of sorting and ordering of data seems an entirely practical task which can be done according to certain technical indexing and cataloguing conventions. Viewed in this way, it seems that once the data are sorted and ordered, the researcher will start to be able to make some interpretive sense of them, and to build their explanations and arguments. However, whilst it is true that the primary sorting and ordering of data in some way or another is a practical necessity, it is not entirely a practical or technical task, and the distinction between this and building analyses and interpretations is thus a blurred one. Cataloguing or indexing systems are not analytically neutral. In other words, in choosing or devising a particular system, you are at the very least making certain assumptions about the kinds of phenomena and units you are cataloguing and the kinds you are not (and indeed what count as data and what do not), as well as how and in what form you will be able to retrieve them later on. In fact you are likely to be making a whole series of further assumptions too, the consequence of which will be to open up some analytical possibilities, and to close off others.

Although it seems obvious to say it, any researcher who intends to sort and organize their data must know what it is that constitutes data in the context of their research. Clearly, you need to have a sense of what it is that you are sorting and organizing before you start, not least because different forms of data will be more or less amenable to different organizing mechanisms. This means that it is vital to revisit the question which you should have asked yourself many times (see especially Chapters 3 and 4):

> What count as data or evidence in relation to my research questions?
> How do I wish to 'read' my data?

Since writing your research design, you may have modified or elaborated your views about what constitute data for your research, or you may have generated unanticipated forms of data. Whether or not this is the case, you will need to engage with all the familiar issues (introduced in Chapters 3 and 4) about how far you wish to 'read' your data *literally*, *interpretively* or *reflexively*.

- If you are intending to 'read' your data *literally*, you will be interested in their literal form, content, structure, style, layout and so on. So, for example, if you are working with interview transcripts, you might be interested in the words and language used, the sequence of interaction, the form and structure of the dialogue, and the literal content. Similarly, if you are working with documents, video, film, visual artefacts, or whatever, a literal reading will mean that you are interested in documenting a literal version of 'what is there'. Whilst you may want to make such literal readings, most qualitative researchers will not want to stop there. Indeed, many would suggest that a purely literal reading is not possible, just as a purely objective description is not possible, because the social world is always already interpreted.

- Whatever your view on the possibility or otherwise of literal readings, you will need to consider to what extent you will want to make an *interpretive* reading of your data. An interpretive reading will involve you in constructing or documenting a version of what you think the data mean or represent, or what you think you can infer from them. You may, for example, read a section of an interview transcript as telling you something about implicit norms or rules with which the interviewee is operating, or discourses by which they are influenced, or something about how discourses are constituted, or as indicating some kind of causal mechanism in social action. You may be mostly concerned with what you see as your interviewees' interpretations and understandings, or their versions and accounts of how they make sense of social phenomena, or you may place more emphasis on your own interpretations. Probably, you will do both to an extent. Whatever form of interpretive reading you adopt, you will be involved in *reading through or beyond* the data in some way, be they literal texts or visual images or whatever.

- Finally, you will need to decide how far you want to make a *reflexive* reading of your data. A reflexive reading will locate you as part of the data you have generated, and will seek to explore your role in the process of generation and interpretation of data. You will probably see yourself as inevitably and inextricably implicated in the data generation and interpretation processes, and you will therefore seek a reading of data which captures or expresses those relationships.

Many qualitative researchers make readings of their data on all three of these levels. In Chapters 3 and 4 we discussed the implications of the different forms of reading for what you actually generate and record as data.

For example, if you wish to read documentary data on all three levels you will need to generate not only literal documents, but also data concerning perhaps the context of their production, consumption, interpretation and use, and data concerning your role in that. The different types of reading have different implications for what you treat as data so that, for example, fieldnotes documenting your own response to a situation, or providing an account of how you interpreted what was happening at the time, how you interpreted it later, and so on, are more likely to be viewed as data in relation to reflexive than literal readings. What this means is that, whatever it is which will be counted as data according to your perspective and the reading you wish to make, this must take a form (or be put into a form) which can be readily sorted and organized for analytical purposes. So, if you have analytical notes and memos, you will need to decide to what extent they can and should constitute data which will be sorted, organized and indexed. If you are using your memories and unrecorded observations as data you need to think critically and honestly about whether you can sort, organize and retrieve these in any meaningful or convincing way, or whether they must first be transformed into text, tape, or diagrams.

In general, you will also need to think about what form it is that the materials which you are working with take. What do the data look or feel like? So, for example, text-based data such as interview transcripts, textual documents, and so on, may take very different forms. A document such as a will, or an Act of Parliament, or an encyclopaedia, may be very formal and standardized. It may be organized into a more or less logical sequence, and already codified to an extent. A semi-structured interview transcript made from an audio tape recording is likely to be much less ordered. It may be disorganized, eclectic, incoherent in places, and may or may not take the form of a sequential narrative. Visual images may be already organized into some form of sequence – indeed you may be interested in that very sequence – such as a film, or photographs on the page of a magazine. Or they may be disorganized, indistinct, unfocused, and so on. Whatever form the materials take, you will need to think about whether or not you wish to work with or against any existing coding, sequencing or organization which has been imposed on the materials, and you will need to think more generally about what their form implies about how you can actually handle them in practice. Do you, for example, need to transform them in some way as part of the process of sorting and organizing them? Do visual images need to be turned into some form of textual description, or can you work with the images themselves?

These are difficult questions, and you may formulate more than one answer in respect of the same piece or set of data for different analytical purposes. Once you have decided what constitute data in your study, and you have some ideas about what form they take and how they therefore need to be handled, you are ready to think about the range of approaches you might take to sorting and organizing them. We will begin with a discussion of what is probably the most commonly used form of data organization.

CROSS-SECTIONAL AND CATEGORICAL INDEXING

Cross-sectional indexing of data involves devising a consistent system for indexing the whole of a data set according to a set of common principles and measures. This technique can also be referred to as 'categorical indexing' to the extent that it uses classificatory categories to establish the common index. The central idea of indexing (some writers and researchers call it categorizing, or coding) is that the researcher applies a uniform set of indexing categories systematically and consistently to their data. These could simply take the form of serial indexing categories, inserted as sub-headings at the relevant points in text-based data, either whilst the text is being produced, or at some stage afterwards. These are likely to function in the same way as headings and subheadings in the chapters of a book, giving a descriptive sense of what each section of text is about, and may be useful as a way of directing the reader's eye around an individual text.

However, there are three main limitations with this form of simple indexing. The first is that although it may be a useful way to signpost the reader in general terms around an individual text, it may produce indexing categories so broad or bland as to be of limited further use, especially for the purposes of making comparisons or connections between more than one text. Secondly, any one piece of qualitative text is likely to address more than one topic or concept at a time, and therefore serial indexing may be inappropriate or impossible to apply. And thirdly, serial indexing is unlikely to work very well in qualitative texts which do not have a uniform layout or follow an ordered sequence, or in non-text-based data. So, for example, it may be more useful for the categorization of texts with a standardized layout such as legal or administrative documents, and less useful for interview transcripts derived from semi-structured conversations or observational fieldnotes.

Even if simple serial indexing is appropriate for some of your analytical purposes, you are likely to want something more sophisticated for other elements. You may want to create indexing categories which can be applied simultaneously to text, where appropriate, and you may want to create more than one type of category (or level of categorization). So, you may end up with a fairly complex set of both unrelated and interrelated categories and subcategories. As far as the logistics of applying the categories indexically is concerned, you will need to devise a system for tagging the appropriate sections of text, or elements of visual images, and so on, with the appropriate category index labels or markers, which can subsequently be used to support the kinds of retrievals you might wish to make. The purpose of this more complex form of indexing is to turn your data into a resource which can be accessed in various ways, according to various purposes. In other words, the function of the categories is to focus and organize the *retrieval* of sections of text, or elements of data, for the purpose of some form of further analysis or manipulation. It is sometimes easier to think of this process as constituting different ways of slicing your data set, for different purposes.

The job of indexing and retrieving text – or slicing your data set – can be done manually, but is much facilitated by the use of custom designed computer software packages (such as QSR NUD·IST, Hypersoft, the Ethnograph, ATLASti). Either way, this involves detailed and time consuming work in creating and applying the indexing categories, but the computer packages will greatly expedite and enhance the retrieval process. We will discuss the mechanics of this kind of process shortly, but first it is important to ask yourself the following question, and to work out what your answers are.

> Do I wish to index my data cross-sectionally in some way? If yes, what are my reasons for wishing to do this?

There are a number of possible answers to this question. Here are some examples of reasons why you are likely to want to engage in some kind of cross-sectional indexing procedure:

- Your data are predominantly text-based. Indexing and retrieval procedures are most readily applied to text-based data, although it is certainly possible to create cross-sectional index systems for visual material like photographs, which might be indexed for example according to the broad subject matter, the camera angle, who took the photographs, their composition, or according to their use, or their positioning within a text. You can index audio and video tape recordings using the tape counter, although quick and complex retrievals are not possible without fairly elaborate equipment or a lot of patience. If you are generating and using visual data, you will need to think carefully about how much cross-sectional indexing you wish to do, and how useful it will be, given that most of the systems and techniques have been devised with text-based data in mind.

- You want to get a systematic overview of your data so that you have a clear idea of their coverage and scope. Engaging in some kind of indexing process – which usually involves amongst other things the systematic and routine scrutiny of one's data – can help the researcher to distance themselves from the immediacy of the initially striking or memorable elements, and therefore to gain a more measured view of the whole. Sorting, organizing and indexing can thus help you to get surprises from your data which take you beyond an impressionistic view based on the limitations of your own memory and your capacity to sort and organize in your head. Of course a researcher can only gain these beneficial effects from the indexing process if they do it themselves, but even if they do not, the index which is produced should itself help them to delineate the scope and coverage of their data. Of course this scope and coverage will be expressed in terms of the indexing categories used, which means that although a researcher may well be able to argue that their overview is systematic, they will not be able to claim that it is the only possible version or way of 'slicing' the data.

- You want to be able to locate and retrieve issues, topics, information, examples and themes which do not appear in an orderly or sequential manner in the data, or in a manner that is easily and straightforwardly visible and accessible. You might want to begin to generate a resource, and a mechanism, which will enable you to select and retrieve elements of your data for the purposes of presentation and dissemination.

- You are beginning the process of creating interpretive, conceptual or analytical categories and themes, and wish to index the location of these in your data. Just as I suggested earlier that the process of indexing helps the researcher to get a sense of the scope and coverage of their data, so this process also can help the researcher in their conceptual, analytical and theoretical thinking.

- You want to establish whether and how well your data address your research questions and your theoretical concerns.

- You think it will give you analytical 'handles' on your data, or ways into your data, so that you can use them (now or later) to decide how to focus your analytical activity, to decide what is relevant and what is not and to develop your explanations and arguments. For example, you may use these 'handles' as a basis for making comparisons or connections within your data. As we shall see shortly, cross-sectional indexing supports some kinds of analyses and explanation building better than others.

- You wish to 'take stock' of your progress in the research process, and assess what to do next. For example, taking stock can mean taking informed decisions about further sampling and data generation (in accordance with principles of theoretical sampling where you analyse your data as they are generated so that you can make further decisions on the basis of the developing analysis and associated theoretical principles: see Chapter 5 for a further discussion of this). Or it can mean taking informed decisions about whether and where to redirect your analytical activity.

It is important to work out which, if any, of these answers apply to your own research, rather than seeing them simply as 'advantages of cross-sectional indexing'. Your reasons for indexing in this way (or indeed for deciding not to do so) will influence the ways in which you do it, as well as what kinds of subsequent analyses you are able to perform.

If you do decide to create a cross-sectional indexing system, you will have to ask yourself:

> What kinds of indexing categories do
> I wish to produce?

This question should direct your attention back towards ontological and epistemological matters. If you do not consider these when you devise your indexing categories, then you are effectively engaging in technique without philosophy, or procedure without strategy, and you are very likely to end up with an indexing system which is inconsistent with the epistemological and ontological core assumptions of your research design.

Ontologically, you will need to be clear about what kinds of phenomena your categories are supposed to represent or constitute instances of. So, for example, if you are creating categories in order to index sections of text, what do these represent? Are they literally only sections of text, or do they represent behaviours referred to in the text, or actions, accounts, attitudes, understandings, practices, discourses, and so on? Are they properties of individuals, institutions, structures, textual practices? Your answers to these questions do not necessarily have to mirror exactly the ontological elements of your research design, since at this stage you are only indexing your data rather than producing your final analysis, but they do of course need to be consistent with them. If you think your categories are simply different elements in an overall story, you nevertheless need to be clear about the ontological terms in which your story, and your categories, are cast because, as I argued in Chapter 2, no research or story can be ontologically neutral.

Epistemologically, you need to think carefully about how your indexing categories represent instances of these ontological phenomena. What kind of knowledge or evidence do they constitute? In particular, are your categories going to be based on literal, interpretive or reflexive readings? If you are creating indexing categories based on literal readings, these might involve the literal substance or form of the text. If you want to produce interpretive and reflexive categories, they are likely to be based on what you think you can infer from sections of the text, or what they imply. This might involve your reading not only what the text actually says, but the implications in your judgement of what is not said, or what is not present literally in the text.

Figure 6.1 illustrates these points using an example of a short piece of an interview transcript, and suggests some literal, interpretive and reflexive indexing categories which might be derived from it.

In effect you will probably want to produce indexing categories in relation to all three levels. The main message is that you must be clear about what each of your categories is intended to represent, so that you can use them consistently and logically. Exactly what you think they represent, and how you therefore intend to use them, must of course also be tied in with the kind of explanatory and analytical logic you intend to rely upon.

> What explanatory or analytical logic does cross-sectional or categorical indexing support?

There is no point in indexing just for the sake of it. You need to ensure that the cross-sectionally indexed chunks or slices of data are going to make some kind of analytical sense. This means that you must think very hard about what your indexed slices of data will look like once they are retrieved, and what kind of explanatory logic they might feed into. For example, if you were to create an indexing category called something like 'inheritance strategies', based on the example given in Figure 6.1, you should think about what such a slice would look like, and what you might do with it. The slice would probably take the form of a collection of all sections of data which had been indexed under the category of inheritance strategies – in that sense it is like a 'bag' of data. What might you do with such a collection? There are two main possibilities, one of which is likely to be more palatable to qualitative researchers than the other.

- Let us begin with the least palatable option. You might treat your slices or bags of categorically indexed data as *variables*. So, for example, you might try to explore relationships between such 'variables' as 'inheritance strategies' and 'rules and norms about right and wrong in inheritance'. Or you might be interested in charting relationships between 'inheritance strategies' and 'gender' by treating these as variables. Usually, variable analysis would involve making inferences about causation or direction and degree of influence based on the apparent associations between variables. I cannot emphasize too strongly, however, that *you must not attempt to do this if you have rejected the logic of variable analysis* (see Chapters 5 and 7 for further discussion of variable analysis), which most qualitative researchers will have done.

- You might alternatively use your slices or bags of indexed data as retrievals which you will treat as *unfinished resources* for a variety of further uses, rather than end products (such as variables) in themselves. For example, you might simply view your slices as ways of seeing thematically across your data set. You might use them to conduct some further analysis, possibly of the content of the slices, or use the slices as a starting point to ask questions which will take you into other parts of your

Figure 6.1   *Examples of literal, interpretive and reflexive indexing categories derived from a section of interview transcript*

The interview transcript

This short section is taken from part-way through a real interview conducted as part of a study of 'Inheritance, Property and Family Relationships' (see Chapter 2, where this project was introduced as an example). There were two interviewees, one male (Robert) and one female (Christine), and a female interviewer (Mary). All of these are pseudonyms. The transcript is a verbatim record of the interaction, although it does not include references to non-verbal behaviour. Short pauses in speech are indicated as (. . .). Interruptions are indicated as //. Words and phrases emphasized by the speaker are underlined. Punctuation has been added, it is hoped in a way which is faithful to the delivery of the dialogue, to make the text more readily intelligible to the reader.

Mary: Have you had other experiences of inheritance in your own family?

Christine: (. . .) Er, um, yes. Well not my own relationships, but my sister, she had um some friends and er the husband was in the ambulance service, right. And the wife, I think she worked actually, so they both contributed towards the household. And they had two children, er, the wife died, which left the husband and the two children. I think the two would be in their late teens, I would think, by then. And this left the husband on his own. Now I think he was left on his own a couple of years and then he met and remarried. And the lady that he married, I think she had a son. And then he got heart trouble, right. And he died when they were away on holiday. And he must have made a will leaving everything to his new wife. So of course his new wife inherited everything that he and his wife had worked to achieve, and his own two children didn't get a ha-penny.

Mary: Oh dear.

Christine: Everything went to the new wife. And so I think it's experiences like that, knowing what happens in those sort of circumstances, that's made me feel like I do about our relationship. And I feel also for Robert's children.

Mary: Yes.

Christine: I think it's wrong that sort of thing, that your own children don't inherit anything. I mean I know it sounds sick that you should feel you've got to leave money and your children need it all, but it's wrong, if you've built a family up and then both mother and father die and the children don't inherit anything from them at all, but some other family inherits it all. It's wrong. And, um, well, that's just my view. Some people maybe think//differently but

Robert: //It is wrong but that's the way it works because unfortunately, when you marry, your next of kin is your wife, whatever relations she had before that. But I think a lot of things are because people don't make contracts before they get married. That's why we don't know when we're getting married because we don't really see much point and purpose at the moment do we?

Christine: Not as we are at the moment, no we're not. I mean what would we gain from getting married?

Suggested literal indexing categories

There are a number of ways in which a piece of transcript like this might be indexed literally. For example, you might wish to index pauses, interruptions, emphasized words, points where one speaker agrees with another, or disagrees, or seems partially to agree but uses that agreement to close a topic and make a separate point (as does Robert when he says 'it is wrong but that's the way it works . . .'), the sequence in which the speakers talk (that is, (1) interviewer, (2) female interviewee, (3) interviewer, (4) female interviewee, (5) interviewer, (6) female interviewee, (7) male interviewee, (8) female interviewee) and so on, especially if you wanted to conduct a fairly detailed form of content analysis. You might want to index what you see as literal topics or points of substance, for example: no personal experience of inheritance; third party experience of inheritance; inheritance and remarriage; inheritance to children; marital status; pre-marital contracts.

Suggested interpretive indexing categories

There is probably an even greater number of ways in which this piece could be indexed interpretively, depending upon the researcher's perspective and interests. Some suggestions of categories related to what you might infer from the transcript, or what you might think it might be telling you in an interpretive sense, are: rules and norms about what is right and wrong in inheritance (especially in the context of remarriage, children, who 'counts' as family, balance — that is, receiving in relation to input); mismatch between law and what people want; inheritance strategies (for example, the strategy of 'not getting married' for these interviewees); inheritance narratives (used to convey normative understandings).

Suggested reflexive indexing categories

On the face of it there seems little to work with reflexively in this section. We do not have any text relating to the researcher's perception of their own role in the interaction, or of their ongoing interpretations of what was going on. However, there are several instances of interviewer empathy or apparent agreement with what is being said. In general, the interviewer is presenting an encouraging response to what Christine is saying, and you might want to categorize each response accordingly for indexing purposes.

data set. This 'unfinished resource' option is likely to be more palatable to qualitative researchers, since it supports a wider range of analytical and explanatory logics than the variable analysis option.

Both of these options suggest a logic of cross-sectional comparison in the formation of explanations, but the former does this in a way which simply extends – probably inappropriately – what is often seen as a quantitative logic of variable analysis into the qualitative domain. This is likely to be inappropriate for a range of reasons, including:

- The treating of indexing categories as though they are variables suggests a high degree of uniformity between each section of data categorized by this label, yet this is unlikely to exist. Whilst your categories should be consistent, they are unlikely to be uniform.

- The idea of a variable may work better for literal readings of data than for interpretive and reflexive readings. Yet qualitative researchers usually wish to engage in one or both of the latter.

- Your indexing categories may refer to complex and/or specific processes which cannot be reduced to a static or simple variable or type, but which are usefully organized under specified indexing headings for you to retrieve and do further analytical work upon.

- The rest of your research design probably does not support this form of analysis. For example, if you have used theoretical sampling, and semi-structured or non-standardized data generation techniques, then these are unlikely to be compatible with this form of variable analysis (see Chapters 3 and 4 on data generation, and Chapter 5 on sampling). This means that, if you try to do some kind of variable analysis, you are unlikely to be able to achieve very effective results.

The kind of cross-sectional comparison supported by the 'unfinished resources' option is less rigid. So, for example, it acknowledges that you may wish to compare all instances of 'inheritance strategies' across your data set, and indeed you might want to explore the relationship between these and 'rules and norms about the rights and wrongs of inheritance'. However, it assists this process by helping you to draw some of the relevant data together – in a bag or slice of data – so that you can explore them further, rather than helping you to manipulate one slice against the other as though they were dependent and independent variables. If you are using cross-sectional indexing according to this logic, you must be very careful that you do not inadvertently find yourself sliding towards the 'variable analysis' way of thinking. As we shall see shortly, some of the computer software packages for analysing qualitative data can encourage you to make this mistake. The following simple rules will help you to resist:

- Do not treat your categorically indexed slices of data as more concrete, uniform or static than you know they are. Do not be tempted to view them as tidy and labelled variables, when you know that they are loose and flexible groupings of unfinished resources which you developed primarily as a retrieval mechanism.

- Do not try to index what cannot be categorized cross-sectionally. For example, it may not be possible to identify and tag complex and specific social processes through a straightforward system of cross-sectional indexing. This might be because they are simply too complex, or too particular, to be encapsulated in an indexing category, or too big to appear in a small chunk of text taken from an interview, a document, or whatever. Or, it might be because they do not appear cross-sectionally in the data set (see discussion of 'non-cross-sectional data organization' later in this chapter). Take, for example, the issue of 'reciprocity' in family relationships. Reciprocity can potentially involve complex systems of exchange, or of give and take, in family life. So, for example, a daughter might receive a financial gift from her father and, although it is defined by both of them as a gift, she might feel a sense of duty to make some repayment for it. The sense of duty is unlikely to come solely from receipt of this particular gift, but will be embedded somehow in the history of the relationship between the daughter and her father, and possibly other relatives. The feeling of duty to repay might contribute to a general feeling of indebtedness towards her father, and the daughter may provide support and assistance to him over many years either directly or indirectly as a consequence of this. Alternatively, she may decide to make a direct repayment which is equivalent in financial terms to the original gift. Or, she may never repay directly, but may always be ready to provide assistance – to be 'on call' if you like – should it be required by her father. There are lots of possible permutations, but the point is that it is unlikely that such a process of reciprocity will be neatly bundled into small chunks of interview text ready for the researcher to categorize and index. Partly, this is because an understanding of reciprocity may come from an interpretive analysis of the 'whole' story, rather than from specific quotations selected from interviews with the daughter or the father. So, whilst a researcher might be 'lucky' enough to be able to identify a chunk of text which does express some form of reciprocity, for example where the daughter talks explicitly about feeling a duty to repay, the very nature of these kinds of social processes means that more often than not they will not come ready packaged in this way. Any one small section of text taken in isolation, or even taken together with others of a similar type, may therefore not express a complex interpretive concept in any meaningful sense. You must think about how useful your indexed slices of data will be before you do the lengthy and time consuming job of indexing and retrieving them.

- Do not forget the context, or interaction, or whatever, which produced the sections of data which you are indexing. It is easy to get carried away with the enthusiasm of designing cross-sectional categorical indexing systems, and to forget that these will have the effect of lifting small sections of data out of their context, so that they can be compared with other similarly decontextualized sections of data. It is possible to cross-sectionally categorize or code certain aspects of context (and some of the computer software packages help you to do this), such as the age or gender of the interviewee, the date of the document, the point in the sequence of the whole text from which your indexed section was extracted, and so on. However, the mechanisms for doing this represent a fairly crude and static way of understanding context and are, of course, based on a logic whereby context can be reduced to certain key characteristics or variables. Indeed, if you were conducting a variable analysis you might wish to conceptualize these as independent variables. You should, therefore, not be satisfied with this as your only mechanism for understanding context, unless you have wholeheartedly and consistently adopted the logic of variable analysis in your study.

Once you have worked out whether and why you might wish to use cross-sectional indexing, you will need to think about how to do it.

> How do I create my indexing
> categories, and how do I apply them
> to my data?

Actually, your first question may be 'where will I get my categories from?' In part, this question is answered by your overall methodological approach and, in particular, whether your study is designed to 'test out' certain clearly formed ideas or hypotheses, or whether you intend to generate ideas, propositions and theories from the data. Putting it this way oversimplifies some complex philosophical and methodological issues (see Chapter 7), but the point really is that some researchers will wish to generate indexing categories in a fairly grounded way on the basis of their ongoing interpretation of their data, whilst others may be less concerned with this. Most researchers within the qualitative tradition fall into the former group, so we will consider what *generating indexing categories from the data* might mean.

In the first place, it means making sure that you are as familiar as you can be with your data – read them, study them, listen to them, think about them and the process of their production, sleep with them under your pillow if you think it will help. However, it also means being very familiar with what I have been calling your intellectual puzzle and with the questions you are attempting to address with your research. You need to ensure that you are categorizing in a way which will produce the right kinds of data slices or bags from your data set. Essentially, you need to create for yourself a mechanism for moving back and forth between your intellectual puzzle, your research questions, and your data, so that you develop your indexing categories through this process of interaction. Keeping to the forefront the question 'where do the categories come from?' – as well as the previous set of questions about what the categories constitute – should help you to ensure that this process is as interactive as you would like it to be. So, for example, if your honest answer has to be that the categories you are developing come entirely from your data with no reference to your research questions, then you can make the appropriate adjustments to your practice.

Using this logic you can start creating indexing categories at any stage in the research process, although I suggest below that you also need to make sure you stop at some point. So, for example, you might start creating categories before you have generated any data, or when you only have a few data. Such categories clearly will be informed mostly by your research questions, and will need to be reworked in the light of the further generation of data. If you are doing a pilot study involving the generation of data, then this might be a very good time to start creating indexing categories – they will assist in the preliminary analysis of your data, and they will give you practice in category creation and indexing.

Ultimately, there is probably no better mechanism for ensuring that the creation of categories is interactive between research questions and data than the process of indexing itself, whether this be at the pilot study stage, or at any point later on. Once you have revisited your research questions, and thoroughly familiarized yourself with your data, it is a good idea to develop a few trial categories, and start a trial run. Once you begin trying to index, not only will you start to discover how sensible and workable (or not) the indexing categories you have seem to be, but also you can simultaneously begin developing new categories and start indexing these too. If you literally keep your research questions nearby while you do this, you can make sure that you are constantly cross-checking between them and your data in the process of developing and applying categories. You should develop notes and records on the construction of the categories while you are doing this, so that you devise a clear set of definitions of what each category constitutes, as well as instructions about how to apply them. These can usefully form the basis of discussions with peers and colleagues about your developing indexing system. However, you must remember that this is a trial run: if your indexing categories are to be systematic and workable they will need to be standardized, and be consistently applied. This implies that at some stage you will need to end the trial run, construct the final list of categories (and definitions, and application instructions), and begin afresh.

Let us now consider *how* you might apply indexing categories to your data. In recent years, techniques for cross-sectionally indexing text-based qualitative data have become more explicitly defined and elaborated, and various computer software applications have been designed to support the indexing and retrieval process (see Dey, 1993; Fielding and Lee, 1991; Miles and Huberman, 1994; Tesch, 1990). Figures 6.2 and 6.3 provide examples of manual and computer assisted systems for indexing and retrieval respectively.

In my view, custom designed computer programs provide invaluable assistance to any qualitative researcher with more than a few texts and documents to index, and it is therefore important to take advantage of them. This is not an unequivocal or universal endorsement though. As suggested in Figure 6.3, many of the functions which computer software packages perform very well actually support the logic of variable analysis, and this may be inappropriate for your qualitative project. Examples of facilities which support this kind of logic are: programs which can trace relationships between indexing categories as used in the text (for example, where

Figure 6.2   *Example of manual, cross-sectional indexing and retrieval system with given categories*

Step 1

Decide what counts as data, for example interview transcripts, fieldnotes, visual images, documents. If possible, make copies of data to work with.

Step 2(a)

Read or scrutinize the data thoroughly, and apply indexing or category codes or labels to appropriate chunks of text, elements of the data, and so on. For text-based data, you might apply these in the margins alongside the appropriate sections of text. For visual images you might apply these literally to the image, or to a set of 'co-ordinates' (such as the lines of latitude and longitude on a map).

Step 2(b)

At the same time, keep a separate record of the location of each entry of the code or label. These are sometimes called identifiers (for example, document name, number and date, page number, paragraph or line number, visual image co-ordinates). If you have simultaneously occurring categories, and subcategories, you may require a system of cross-referencing (that is, for other categories which apply to that piece of text).

Step 3

Retrieval then involves using the indexes to locate whatever it is you want in the data, and going back to the originals – just as you would thumb through the index of a book and then flick to the appropriate pages. Or, with text-based data you can make copies of the originals and cut and paste them into category files, although this can waste a lot of trees. This is very time consuming, and unwieldy, since it generally involves having lots of different files and papers open simultaneously on your desk. If you wish to explore connections and overlaps between categories, there are very real physical and temporal limitations on how far you can get. For example, imagine you want to look at the relationship between material coded by three of your categories, in 60 interview transcripts, 200 pages of fieldnotes, and 100 legal documents. You need a very large desk and a lot of patience.

---

categories occur simultaneously, or in a particular sequence); or between 'base data' or social characteristics (for example, age, gender, social class of interview respondents) and indexing categories; and those which offer the facility of building trees or hierarchies of indexing categories to help you to develop explanations of the relationships between the categories (this kind of facility is often referred to in the software manuals and marketing materials as 'theory building'). Whilst it is possible, probably, to use all these facilities without engaging in variable analysis, the programs can be quite seductive and give the researcher a false impression that they are actually dealing with neatly packaged variables. If you are considering using a software package for the computer analysis of qualitative data you should be aware that apparently technical details such as these do support specific epistemological, analytical and explanatory strategies. You should therefore examine carefully what the software manufacturers or distributors say

Figure 6.3   *Example of computer assisted cross-sectional indexing and retrieval system with given categories*

Step 1

Enter texts and documents into computer in a form appropriate for the software package you wish to use. You should enter at this stage any identifying names or numbers and other general information. Texts which you produce yourself (for example, fieldnotes or interview transcripts) can be typed directly into the computer. Other texts or documents can possibly be retyped into the computer (in full or in summary), machine read, or kept 'off line'. The latter option means that only your index, rather than the documents to which it refers, will be handled by computer, and this may be the most feasible method of indexing visual data which has not been transformed into a text-based format.

Step 2

Read the texts thoroughly (either on screen or off) and use the system provided by the software for entering indexing or category codes alongside appropriate chunks of text within the computer program. If you are not sure how much text to index each time, it is probably best to be a little over-inclusive (especially if you are using indexing to create 'unfinished resources' rather than 'variables'), because longer retrieved slices will make more sense when viewed out of the context of the whole text than will shorter ones. The computer cannot create the categories for you, or decide to which chunks of text they apply – unless your categories are literal such as, for example, particular words or phrases which appear in the text, and for which the computer can search. Most qualitative researchers cannot rely entirely on such word searches, since their indexing categories are too conceptual or interpretive for this simple method. For text-based documents which have been entered into the computer, custom designed software packages will automatically attach the appropriate identifiers to your indexing categories (for example name, number and date of document, page, paragraph or line number) so you do not need to keep a separate record of these.

Step 3

Retrieval then involves using the computer program to locate and call up (on screen or in print) whatever it is you want from the text. Custom designed programs will automatically label each chunk of text with appropriate identifiers, and some of them will attach other notes and produce statistical information if you wish. As well as producing retrievals much more quickly and efficiently than you can do manually, the capacity and sophistication of the retrieval programs arguably transform – not just expand and hasten – what it is that you are able to do. Many of the programs offer fairly elaborate retrieval options, enabling you to trace connections, overlaps and relationships – sometimes called Boolean searches – between indexing categories. Beware though: although it can be very useful to make retrievals based on the simultaneous appearance of two or more indexing categories if you are planning to use the retrieved material as an 'unfinished resource', ask yourself how far what the software actually offers implies a logic of variable analysis which may be inappropriate for your research.

about how the program works. Above all, what you must check is that your approach to epistemology and explanation is consistent with (or at least complementary to) the one underlying the software.

There are further difficult questions about indexing categories with which you will need to engage, as follows.

> When should I make final decisions about what the indexing categories will be?

> When should I start indexing?

> When should I finish?

> How many times should I index my data?

The strategies of generating indexing categories at least in part from data on the one hand, and producing consistent cross-sectional categories on the other, can seem rather contradictory. The one suggests sensitivity to data and a high degree of flexibility – for example to reinterpret categories, to create new categories at any stage in the process – and the other suggests a higher degree of rigidity, at least once a final set of categories has been decided upon. But as I suggested earlier, if your data slices or bags are to make sense and be useful, you will need to introduce standardization at some stage. It is therefore important to keep in mind the question 'when do I make final decisions about what the indexing categories will be?' The temptations to delay the final decision about indexing categories are great and this question is useful not least as a constant reminder that you do have to make such final decisions. If you do not, you may waste a lot of time and effort producing an indexing system which is so *ad hoc* as to be useless. Or, you may spend so long developing and refining your list of indexing categories, that you leave yourself far too little time for the painstaking business of actually doing the indexing, and the retrievals, and working with the products to produce your explanations and arguments.

Indexing and retrieval is a very time consuming and labour intensive business, whether or not you use a computer software package. Indeed, although such packages undoubtedly speed up and enhance the process of retrieval, they arguably do not actually decrease the amount of time you spend on this both because they make possible more ways of retrieving, and because they tend to encourage the researcher to develop a greater number of indexing categories in the first place. There is, of course, no point in having a perfectly refined list of categories if you do not have time to index your data with all of them, or if you do not have the time or resources to do all the retrievals that you want to, and to analyse further the products of these retrievals. Do not underestimate how long indexing, retrieval and further analysis will take you. A trial run can be useful in helping you to calculate this fairly precisely (it will depend on the number and complexity of your categories, the nature and quantity of your data, and so on). Do not make plans to categorize your data more than once (unless using the facility some software packages offer for automatically subdividing or adding original categories to make new ones) unless you have very good reasons for doing so, because this may represent a very large investment of time for a procedure which is ultimately likely to constitute only one limited part of your total analytical effort.

> How many indexing categories do I need to produce? How will I know whether I have the right number?

As well as asking yourself questions about the nature of your categories, and the timing of the indexing process, you also need to think about whether you are producing a sensible number of categories for your analytical purposes. If you have too few categories, you may end up with what you feel is a sketchy and inadequate indexing system – just like a book index which has only half of the relevant items within it. Given that you will be wanting to do further work on the retrieved slices or bags of data, you will have to accept that if they are not focused sufficiently around core issues (because you have cast your categories too generally or broadly), or if there are not slices for all of the core issues (because you have missed some out), then you will have problems at that stage. The first problem is easier to deal with than the second, since it simply means that you may wish to do some sharpening or refining, and possibly some subcategorizing. Although these all represent investments of time and effort, they are possible, and may actually help you in the process of building explanations and arguments. On the other hand, if you have entirely overlooked some important categories, and you do need cross-sectional data slices for these, then you will have no choice but to do without them, or to index the whole data set again with your new categories.

However, if you have too many categories, you will also have problems. If you have simply included some categories which you subsequently decide are irrelevant, then the problem is only that you have wasted time and effort in indexing them. But if you have produced a set of categories which are too precise and too refined at too early a stage, then they may be less useful than you had hoped. So, for example, an interview-based study of geographical migration might, in your view, require an analysis of different types of residential move. You might perhaps think that moves which involve short geographical distances are qualitatively different from those involving long distances, and be tempted to produce indexing categories such as: short distance moves; medium distance moves; long distance moves. You would then try to index your interview transcripts or notes using these categories, so that every mention of a short, medium or long distance move can be retrieved and collected together in three data bags. There are a number of problems with this however. First, in order to ensure consistency you would presumably need to specify, perhaps using a linear measurement like kilometres or miles, exactly what you meant by short, medium and long. Yet the precise distance of a move might not always be made clear in each section of text which nevertheless refers, broadly, to geographical distance. Alternatively you might use your interviewees' understandings of what constitutes a short, medium or long distance move rather than a linear measurement, but you would consequently have to accept that where one interviewee might see 50 kilometres as a short distance, another might see it as a long distance. So, although you could categorize every section of text where short, medium and long term moves (in your interviewees' terms) are mentioned, you may not be indexing like with like in terms of linear distance. You would also still have the problem that discussions about distance which do not refer specifically to short, medium or long distances would not be indexed by this system, yet presumably would be relevant to your analysis. Secondly, if you were to use a linear measurement of distance, you may find that the interval you have chosen between short, medium and long is much too big, or much too small. This could result in nearly every type of move being categorized as, say, long distance, simply because they were all in excess of 50 kilometres. Thirdly, and most importantly, you are unlikely to get a qualitative and conceptual sense of how people perceive or construct geographical distance, or of what part it might play in their thinking about residential moves, with such a system. What people count as short, medium or long distance might vary not just between different interviewees, but also for the same interviewees in different contexts or at different times in their lives. People may think of distances in ways other than linear measurements or lengths, such as the ease with which they can travel between one point and another, the cost of the journey, and so on. If you index using categories based on short, medium and long distance criteria, you will probably miss all kinds of interesting discussions and inferences about distance, and instead you will simply end up with a bag or slice of data based on one way of conceptualizing distance. In this example, therefore, you would probably find that it is better to use the more open and flexible indexing category of 'distance', to index all instances of talk about anything to do with distance in relation to residential moves, than to fine tune your indexing category from the beginning into short, medium and long distance. Subsequently of course, if you wanted to, you could explore the contents of your 'distance' data bag in order to develop an understanding of different ways of understanding distance, including, perhaps, short, medium and long distance. This example shows why thinking ahead to what each bag or slice of categorized chunks of data will look like is really important, because it can help you to make workable initial decisions about the scope and shape of your categories. Ultimately, what you choose to do will depend again on what you expect your categories to do for you, and what kind of explanatory logic you are going to apply in your data analysis.

> ## Have I made the best use of available technology?

I have made various points about the use of custom designed computer software throughout this section, and clearly individual researchers will need to assess for themselves how useful these packages might be for their own purposes (see Miles and Huberman, 1994, Appendix, for a useful if brief review of the capabilities of different software packages; see also 'further reading' at the end of this chapter). I have already suggested that you should scrutinize the published information about any programs you are considering using to check whether they are compatible with your approach to epistemology, and of course you must also check more generally that the program will help you to do what you want to do, and that you have the appropriate equipment and so on to run it. It is a very good idea to speak to other researchers who have used a program, and there are various formal and informal networks of users both nationally and internationally which you could explore. Overall, it is important to ask yourself whether you are making the best use of the technology available to you though, and this applies equally to enthusiasts and to those who feel uncertain about, or resistant to, the merits of computers. For enthusiasts, you should ask yourself whether you are placing too great an emphasis on what the software can do, to the point where this is driving your analytical activity and epistemology rather than being driven by them. Many of the packages offer a range of 'quantitative' facilities, such as percentage calculations of text indexed by specified themes, and some of them make big claims about their 'theory building' capabilities. However, these are usually based on a logic of variable analysis or a mode of quantification which may be entirely inappropriate both for your overall methodological stance, and for the specific nature of the project which you have conducted (in terms of its sampling, methods of data generation, and so on). If that is so, you must ensure that your enthusiasm for the technology does not cloud your research judgement about what is useful and what is not in the context of your project. If, on the other hand, you are uncertain about the value of computer analysis, you should ask yourself whether you have made an adequate survey of what is available, and whether or not you are avoiding the use of technology unnecessarily. It is very useful for indexing and retrieval – activities which most qualitative researchers probably engage in – even for a relatively small number of documents, texts, transcripts, and so on (which can still produce a large mass of data).

I have devoted much of my discussion of the sorting and organization of qualitative data to these cross-sectional forms of indexing, because they are very commonly used and also because it is important, in my view, to spell out the potential dangers of using them as though they are a form of variable analysis. There are, however, at least two other ways of organizing and sorting qualitative data, and it is to a brief discussion of these that we shall now turn.

NON-CROSS-SECTIONAL DATA ORGANIZATION

As we have seen, the logic of cross-sectional data indexing is that you devise the same set of indexing categories for use, cross-sectionally, across the whole of your data set. In other words, you are using the same lens to explore patterns and themes which occur across your data. Non-cross-sectional forms of data organization involve ways of seeing and sorting your data which do not necessarily use the same lens across the whole in this way. Essentially, non-cross-sectional data organization involves looking at discrete parts, bits or units within your data set, and documenting something about those parts specifically. In that sense, it is a practice guided by a search both for the *particular* rather than the common or consistent, and the *holistic* rather than the cross-sectional. Every qualitative researcher should ask themselves the following question.

> Do I wish to organize my data in a non-cross-sectional way? If yes, what are my reasons for wishing to do this?

There are a number of possible answers to this question. Here are some examples.

- You want to gain a sense of the distinctiveness of different parts or elements of your data set, which a search for common cross-sectional themes might not provide.

- You wish to understand intricately interwoven parts of your data set, or social processes, or complex narratives or practices, for example, and you believe that these are too complicated or elaborate to be amenable to categorical indexing (or at least to be usefully indexed in this way).

- You wish to organize data around themes, issues or topics which do not appear cross-sectionally in your data set because, for example, they are particular, specific or idiosyncratic.

- You think this method of data organization will provide the most appropriate form of analytical 'handle' on your data, enabling you to make comparisons and to build explanations in a distinctive way. We shall examine, shortly, what kind of analytical logic non-cross-sectional indexing supports.

- You wish to use this method in addition to, for example, cross-sectional indexing, so that you can build explanations based on two alternative ways of 'slicing' your data set. Most qualitative researchers would be unhappy simply to adopt cross-sectional indexing, and will want to also use non-cross-sectional forms of data organization.

> ## How should I go about non-cross-sectional data organization?

In order to answer this question you will need to decide what are the meaningful data organizing principles and data 'units' in the context of your research project, and you will of course have to engage with the question of whether you are reading your data literally, interpretively or reflexively (see above). Examples of non-cross-sectional organizing principles are: case studies, stories, narratives, biographies, and other 'holistic' sequences. Examples of units might be people, documents, laws and policies. The term 'case study' is perhaps rather imprecise, and could probably be used to describe all of the other organizing principles in the list. In a useful review of case study methods, Yin says that 'the case study allows an investigation to retain the holistic and meaningful characteristics of real-life events – such as individual life cycles, organizational and managerial processes, neighbourhood change, international relations, and the maturation of industries' (1989: 14). You do not have to see yourself as doing 'case study research' to be able nevertheless to identify case studies within your data set for analytical purposes. Whilst non-cross-sectional data organization does not have to be done around 'real life events', this is certainly one of the commonly used principles. Equally, however, you might identify 'holistic sequences' which do not map directly onto real life events.

Just as with cross-sectional indexing, and the resultant data bags or slices, you will need to think about what kind of sense your data will make once organized non-cross-sectionally around the principles you have chosen. So, for example, does it make sense to collate and prepare data on the individual biographies of some of the interviewees in your study, or some of the participants in your setting? Would a case study which charts the emergence, construction and context of a particular law be meaningful? Would a detailed analysis of the layout and style of a particular visual image be helpful?

If the answer to these questions is yes, then your task is to begin to organize your data around the principles you have identified. You will probably do this manually, since the computer software packages for analysing qualitative data for the most part are designed to assist cross-sectional categorical indexing. Nevertheless, you might use a database or computer graphics package to help you to construct and represent sequences in your data. You may well wish to construct diagrams and charts (see next section for a fuller discussion). Your task will be to identify and represent what you see as the key elements of the *particular* and *holistic* part of your data which you are examining. Just as the creation of cross-sectional indexing categories should be done as a reflexive practice, where you document the steps in your thinking and in the final definitions of each category, so too with non-cross-sectional methods you should be clear about what organizing principles you are using to identify the key elements of each particular and holistic part. Do not let the use of terms like 'holistic' and 'real life events' allow you to forget that every narrative or representation is a *version* rather than an objective and neutral description. You will be using a set of principles derived from somewhere, and it is important that you are clear about what these are and where they come from.

> What explanatory or analytical logic does non-cross-sectional data organization support?

Non-cross-sectional data organization supports an analytical logic whereby explanations are derived from analysis and comparison of holistic 'units' or elements (such as biographies, organizational histories, and so on), rather than parts, slices or themes (or indeed variables) compared cross-sectionally (such as sections of data derived from interview transcripts relating to the theme 'inheritance strategies'). This means that the researcher begins by analysing the holistic 'unit', or case study, to try to produce an explanation of processes, practices, or whatever, within that unit. This might, for example, involve an analysis of someone's biography and an explanation of how they came to be in a position where they inherited a large sum of money from a relative, or indeed it might involve an explanation of inheritance strategies they had used throughout their life. Instead of then moving on to examine another unit (or biography) and to compare its features as though they were like for like with the first unit, the researcher compares the *explanation* of the first unit with the *explanation* of the second, both explanations having been derived from a holistic rather than cross-sectional analysis. I have used the same thematic example as that used to discuss cross-sectional indexing – that is, inheritance and inheritance strategies – to illustrate that it is possible to approach similar substantive intellectual issues from these different analytical directions. Indeed, it is common to use both approaches in tandem, especially given the limited explanatory potential of cross-sectional data organization for many of the questions about social process, and interpretive and qualitative complexity with which qualitative researchers frequently wish to grapple.

DIAGRAMS AND CHARTS

Finally, I want to say a few words about the use of diagrams and charts in the process of data sorting and organization. In fact, you might use these as a tool in their own right, or as an aid to both cross-sectional and non-cross-sectional forms of organization. They might take the form of diagrammatical or graphical recordings or representations of data, of the cross-sectional or non-cross-sectional organization of your data, or of your analysis as it develops. Let us begin with the standard question which you should ask.

> Do I wish to organize my data diagrammatically? If yes, what are my reasons for wishing to do this?

Among the possible answers to this question are:

- You may use diagrams to record or represent your data, because it may be easier or quicker to 'read' them in that way. So, for example, you may draw diagrams of spatial layouts, or of sequences of interaction, or you might use flow charts to represent sequences of events.

- You might wish to construct diagrams or charts as an analytical tool to help you in your analytical thinking. If you do this, you may or may not actually use the diagrams in any presentation of your data to third parties. Sometimes, using diagrams in this way can help you to spot connections or relationships in your data which are difficult to 'see' when data are in, for example, a text-based format. A good example of this is in the use of charts to plot the relationship between different types of time in the study of 'life courses' (see Hareven, 1982, for an example of this). These can be used to show, simultaneously in chronological sequence, events which take place in historical time (for example, wars, droughts, changes of government), family time (for example, marriages, births, deaths), and individual time (for example, job changes, earnings, education, health). You might have gained data on these three types of time from various sources, and plotting them together on one chart can help you to spot potential connections between them which might not have been visible from the perspective of any one of the sources.

• You might create diagrams or charts of your cross-sectional indexing categories, or of your non-cross-sectional forms of data organization. These might be fairly simple, or you might want to develop some kind of flow chart or matrix of relationships between the different elements. Some of the software packages for analysing qualitative data do encourage you to chart relationships between indexing categories spatially, although as I suggested earlier you should beware the logic of variable analysis which tends to underpin this kind of activity.

• You may wish to use diagrams, charts and graphs as presentation or display tools. This might be because they are simply more eye-catching, or because they make complex material easier to understand.

Whichever of these reasons applies, you are likely to be using diagrammatical forms of data organization alongside one or both of the other types discussed earlier.

> How should I go about
> diagrammatical organization of data?

There are very many different ways of constructing diagrams, charts and graphs in the analysis of qualitative data (see Miles and Huberman, 1994, for an excellent discussion), and the increased availability of fairly sophisticated computer technology enhances the possibilities. The key guiding principle, as with other forms of data organization, is to think about what job it is that you expect diagrams to do for you, and what your data will look like when organized in this way. Therefore, you should ask yourself why you are producing diagrams, and as a consequence think about how to do it.

Diagrams, charts and graphs can be organized around a range of 'axes', dimensions or principles, just as cross-sectional indexing categories or holistic units can be, and you need to make sure that the ones you are working with are meaningful in the context of your own project, its research questions, and the methodology you have adopted. You will, of course, have to decide whether the diagrams are to be organized around literal, interpretive or reflexive readings of your data. For example, a literal diagram might involve a map of the spatial layout of a setting in which you are conducting observation. An interpretive diagram might take the form of a 'cognitive map' which charts what you reckon to be, perhaps, the reasoning process of one of your interviewees. A reflexive diagram might do this in relation to your own reasoning process. In thinking about the axes, dimensions or principles which underlie your diagrams, it can be easy to muddle the literal, interpretive and reflexive dimensions. For example, one form of diagram which is extensively used in social research is the family tree. At first glance you may think that a family tree is a literal diagram, because it charts literal family relationships or kinship positions. However, family trees can be drawn differently according to the formal conventions used for understanding so-called blood and kin relationships, and some cultural ways of understanding kinship are very difficult to reproduce as a 'tree' at all. A family tree may look different depending upon which set of formal conventions you are following, and upon whether you are using what you see as your research subject or interviewee's own understandings of kinship. Both of these suggest that you will be playing with interpretive, rather than literal, readings of data, in the construction of your diagram. You should, therefore, make sure that you are clear about where your interpretive principles have come from.

> What explanatory or analytical logic does diagrammatical data organization support?

Diagrams, charts and graphs can support a wide range of explanatory logics, including both of those we have discussed already in this chapter, as well as a logic which does not depend on the use and manipulation of text as an underpinning principle. However, different ways of composing and drawing diagrams will suggest specific explanatory logics, and you must be aware of these when making your diagrammatic choices. Flow charts, for example, suggest a linear or sequential logic of explanation, and to some extent probably depend on the use of categorical indexing, or at least the application of categorical labels to sections of data. Most diagrams which are reproduced on paper are two-dimensional (or at least can only mimic three-dimensionality), which may restrict their explanatory potential.

CONCLUSION

In this chapter we have examined the three most commonly used forms of qualitative data organization. Whilst these represent very important parts of the analytical process, I have been careful not to suggest that they constitute the whole act of data analysis in themselves. In a sense, all that these methods do is to help you to organize and 'get a handle' on your data. The remainder of your analytical effort will go into constructing explanations in relation to your intellectual puzzle, and in working out how to present these to others in a convincing way. The construction of convincing explanations, including questions about how this should be done, what should be seen as convincing, and so on, is one of the most contested areas of debate in the social sciences. It is a difficult area for qualitative researchers, who very often find themselves going against the grain of conventional modes of thought. It is therefore to these questions and issues that we shall turn in the next chapter.

FURTHER READING

Atkinson, P. (1990) *The Ethnographic Imagination*, London: Routledge (this is not a technical 'how-to-do-it' text, but provides a useful discussion of different ways of 'reading' ethnography)

Ball, M.S. and Smith, G.W.H. (1992) *Analyzing Visual Data*, London: Sage

Bryman, A. and Burgess, R.G. (eds) (1994) *Analyzing Qualitative Data*, London: Routledge

Burgess, R.G. (ed.) (forthcoming) *Qualitative Methodology and Computing*, London: Falmer Press

Dey, I. (1993) *Qualitative Data Analysis: a User-Friendly Guide for Social Scientists*, London: Routledge (on computer aided cross-sectional and diagrammatical organization of data)

Fielding, N.G. and Lee, R.M. (eds) (1991) *Using Computers in Qualitative Research*, London: Sage

Hammersley, M. (1990) *Reading Ethnographic Research: a Critical Guide*, London: Longman

Miles, M.B. and Huberman, A.M. (1994) *Qualitative Data Analysis: an Expanded Sourcebook*, 2nd edn, London: Sage (an excellent all-round resource with lots of ideas for the organization and sorting of qualitative data)

Scott, J. (1990) *A Matter of Record: Documentary Sources in Social Research*, Cambridge: Polity

Silverman, D. (1993) *Interpreting Qualitative Data: Methods for Analyzing Talk, Text and Interaction*, London: Sage

Strauss, A. and Corbin, J. (1990) *Basics of Qualitative Research: Grounded Theory Procedures and Techniques*, London: Sage (on techniques specific to grounded theory in the Glaser and Strauss, 1967, tradition)

Tesch, R. (1990) *Qualitative Research: Analysis Types and Software Tools*, London: Falmer

Yin, R.K. (1989) *Case Study Research: Design and Methods*, London: Sage (Chapter 5 'Analyzing Case Study Evidence')

7

PRODUCING ANALYSES AND EXPLANATIONS WHICH ARE CONVINCING

In the last chapter we explored ways in which qualitative researchers might begin to sort and organize their data, and gave some suggestions about the types of analyses or explanations building which the different methods might support. We emphasized that organizing and sorting are not conceptually neutral activities, and that you must be aware of the kinds of analytical and explanatory possibilities not only that you open up, but also that you close off, by organizing your data in certain ways. In this chapter we will examine much more thoroughly what kinds of analyses and explanations you are likely to want to develop – and indeed to be able to develop – on the basis of your qualitative data. We will then go on to ask how you might ensure that your analyses and explanations are *convincing* and, as a part of that discussion, we will explore tricky questions about the reliability, validity and generalizability of qualitative data analyses. Producing a convincing argument or explanation involves, amongst other things, successfully presenting and disseminating your data analyses, and so questions about how you convince not only yourself, but also a wider audience, will be addressed. Finally, we will tackle some of the key issues in the ethics and politics of qualitative data analysis and presentation.

BUILDING EXPLANATIONS AND ANALYSES

I have argued earlier that I see qualitative researchers as being in the business of producing social explanations, or addressing intellectual puzzles. However, in Chapter 2 I also suggested that there are different types of social explanations. You will have designed a study which is likely to be able to help you to produce certain types of explanations and not others, and you need to be clear about what the possibilities are. This can be expressed in terms of the following difficult question about social explanation and analysis:

> What kinds of social explanations or
> arguments can I build from my data?
> And conversely, what kinds of social
> explanations are outside the scope of
> my analysis?

In answering this question you must start to make direct links between your current analytical thoughts, your original research design, your research questions, and your intellectual puzzle. In other words you must revisit those difficult questions about what your research is really about, what it is that you really want to know, and so on. Your research questions will have suggested particular types of social explanations and, if you have designed and conducted a study which really does address those questions through the use of appropriate methods, sampling and so on, then you must now also produce explanations which are meaningful in relation to those questions. If you have modified your research questions throughout the research process, then you need to establish clearly what questions you currently are aiming to answer so that you can concentrate on developing the right kinds of social explanations in relation to them.

How do you decide what are the right kinds of explanations, however? As with other key aspects of the research process, the first step is to recognize that there *are* different types of social explanations, albeit the categorizations of these can be both ambiguous and confusing, and are certainly contested within the social sciences (see Blaikie, 1993; Harding, 1986; Hughes, 1990; Rose, 1994; Stanley and Wise, 1993). It is not my purpose to prescribe particular forms of social explanations as being the best or most worthy *per se*, or to tell you how you should conceptualize and distinguish between them, but instead to inspire you to work this out for yourself, in the context of the ontological and epistemological frameworks you have fashioned for your own research. Let us therefore consider some difficult questions about the different ways in which social explanations can be conceptualized in relation to qualitative research, along a number of key dimensions.

> What is my explanation doing? What
> explanatory logic is it using? Do my
> data allow this?

Social explanations can do different things, and you will need to be aware of what you are expecting yours to do, and to be certain that you have generated appropriate data to enable this to be done. Here are some possible answers to the question of what your explanation is doing, and what explanatory logic it is using.

- comparing. You may wish to develop an explanation which explicitly compares social phenomena, social processes, social locations, social meanings, and so on. *Comparative explanations* will aim to draw some explanatory significance from a specified set of comparisons. In other words, the logic of explanation will be tied up with the mechanism of comparison. If you are constructing a comparative explanation, you will need to ask yourself whether you have generated data on the key comparative components, and whether the data are actually comparable (they do not have to be identical) in ways which are useful for the development of an explanation.

- developing and tracing. *Developmental explanations* are those which attempt to trace and account for the development of social phenomena, social processes, social change and so on. Here, the logic of explanation is centred on the idea that a meaningful process of development, or a story, or a narrative, can be invoked. If you are constructing a developmental explanation, you will need to ask yourself whether your data enable you to trace or chart relevant developmental stages or issues, and whether you have accessed these in a form which can usefully be woven together in explanatory fashion.

- describing. *Descriptive explanation* is a rather vague term and, in order to be useful, needs further modification. A descriptive explanation may involve the construction of some kind of explanatory account of what is going on in a particular social location, or of the operation of a set of social processes. However, the idea that 'pure', neutral, atheoretical or objective description can be achieved has been much criticized by qualitative researchers (see for example Hammersley, 1992). If you are intending to produce a descriptive explanation, you will need to be very clear about what you have selected as the relevant explanatory factors, and on which 'hooks' or 'pegs' you are hanging your description. And of course you will need to ask yourself whether you have generated data relevant to these hooks and pegs.

- predicting. *Predictive explanations* are those where the logic of explanation is tied in with conventions for predicting social phenomena. So, for example, your predictive explanation may be based on the principle that, if it is possible to observe what happened under certain specified conditions in a certain social location, then you may be able to predict what might happen in the future under similar conditions, or where conditions are different in certain known ways. If you are developing a predictive explanation you will need to be clear about what conventions and criteria for prediction you are using and, as with the other examples, you will need to ask yourself whether you have indeed generated data which fulfil these criteria.

• theorizing. My use of the term *explanation* implies that any qualitative data analysis should have a wider relevance to some explanatory body of knowledge or social interpretation, and in that sense all of the forms of explanation I have discussed are *theoretical explanations*. In my view, explanations cannot (and should not attempt to) be atheoretical, and it is therefore not very useful to ask yourself whether or not you are constructing a theoretical explanation. However, there are different ways of conceiving the relationship between theory construction and the research process, as well as different ways of understanding the role and significance of theory for the social sciences. The former concerns the kinds of materials which researchers use to construct explanations and theories in relation to their own data, and we shall examine this shortly. The latter involves the mechanisms and confidence with which researchers connect their analyses with larger or wider forms of theorizing, and we shall explore these issues in the section on 'convincing yourself and others'.

Trying to understand the concept of explanation in terms of what the explanation is *doing*, or what is the explanatory logic, produces these types of distinctions, and I think they are useful in helping to concentrate the researcher's mind on what type of explanation they are able to, and wish to, produce. The categories are not, however, mutually exclusive, and many explanations contain elements of more than one. For example, a predictive explanation may be based on a combination of comparative and developmental explanatory logic. Moreover, whichever type or types of explanation(s) you are constructing along this dimension, you will also have to engage with a further set of issues which are encapsulated in the following questions.

> According to what kind of reasoning, and with what materials, is my explanation constructed?

> Specifically, what is the role of empirical data *per se* in the explanation I am constructing?

> Do my data, and does my research practice, enable me to construct an explanation in this way?

These questions direct our attention to the role of empirical data, and of the research process, in the fashioning of social explanations. In moving towards finding the relevant answers for your research project, the first step – as with the question about different kinds of social explanations – is to recognize that different answers are possible. Let us consider some of the different versions.

- The first version of an answer to these questions involves whether you see your data as constituting the explanation in themselves, or whether your data provide a way into an explanation, or represent or signify an explanation. In other words, to what extent do you need to interpret your data, or read behind or beyond them, in order to produce the materials necessary to construct your explanation? The key question to ask yourself here is:

> Do my data constitute evidence in themselves in a literal or circumstantial sense, or do they stand for or represent evidence of something else in an interpretive or significative sense?

For example, your view may be that empirical observations, or events, or patterns can demonstrate connections, causal correlations, explanations or even laws in and of themselves. In other words, if you can chart the circumstantial connections between, say, empirical variables, then these *in themselves* will constitute your explanation. This 'variable analysis' view of course fits with a classic positivist version of social science research, and is unlikely to encapsulate everything that a qualitative researcher would wish to do, as we saw in the previous chapter. Alternatively, you may consider that such empirical patterns are not useful so much in themselves, as because they can provide circumstantial evidence for *underlying processes* or causal mechanisms which are not explicitly manifest in the empirical patterns themselves. This would be broadly consistent with a realist view of social science research (and indeed a realist critique of variable analysis: see Pawson, 1989). In this view, you would be saying that empirical observations can be explained by underlying mechanisms which are not directly observable in themselves. Or, you may consider that interpretations of meanings, experiences, accounts, actions, events, can be developed into explanations and understandings and indeed that other analytical logics such as variable analysis make no sense because they exclude these dimensions (see

Blumer, 1956, for the classic interpretivist critique of variable analysis). According to this, broadly interpretivist view, the role of the researcher is to understand everyday or *lay interpretations*, as well as supplying *social science interpretations*, and to move from these towards an explanation.

Whatever your answer to this question, you must consider whether or not you are organizing, sorting and analysing your data in ways which are consistent with that answer. If, for example, your answer locates you towards the interpretivist position, then you need to make sure that, amongst other things, you are indeed searching your data for, and organizing them around, relevant interpretive categories or themes. You will need to develop transparent and systematic mechanisms for arriving at your interpretations, and for drawing on lay interpretations.

- The second answer to this overall set of questions centres on the extent to which you view 'the empirical' as having an independent existence from the research endeavour. Although the different approaches to the question of whether data are literal or significative are distinctive, and represent differing degrees of interpretation, or of moving behind or beyond data, I have also argued quite strongly in previous chapters for a position which sees data as the product of processes of generation and interpretation in which the researcher is inevitably implicated. I am suggesting, therefore, that data cannot exist in an uninterpreted form, but you will need to engage with this question yourself, in relation to your own research. Specifically:

> Does the empirical exist
> independently of my attempts to
> explain it, and can I construct a
> neutral or independent explanation?

Most qualitative researchers would probably answer 'no' to this question, and certainly the second half of it, favouring a view that the social world is 'always already interpreted', and can only be 'known' by socially located 'knowers' (be they social scientists, or non-social-scientist social actors). This can be contrasted with the view that social reality is made up of social facts which can be observed independently as empirical patterns, regularities, and irregularities. The middle route would suggest that an empirical or 'real world' does exist independently, but that it can only be known and understood interpretively.

Again, you will need to ensure that your methods of data generation, and your research practice in general, enable you to adopt the appropriate forms of data analysis here. So, for example, if you agree with the interpretivist view that 'knowers' are centrally implicated in the production of knowledge, then you must make sure that you have generated the means and materials necessary to understand that process and the interpretations of the 'knowers'. If you have conducted a questionnaire survey whose logic is premised on the assumption that data objectively exist 'out there', and can be neutrally collected using standard research tools, then you will be unlikely to have generated the appropriate materials for an interpretive explanation. What you will need are data and materials which can help you to develop a systematic and transparent way of understanding and interpreting what you have generated from 'knowers' in your research, and that is likely to include evaluating your own role in the production of knowledge from your research.

• The third version of an answer concerns at what point in the research process the construction and development of theory is done, and therefore involves the further question:

> When and how should the
> construction and development of
> theory take place in the research
> process?

There are at least three possible answers, and they link in with different philosophical positions in the social sciences.

1   Theory comes first, before empirical research and analysis, and is tested on or measured against data. The theory is not derived from data in this version, except in the sense of having been refined through previous studies which may have confirmed or refuted earlier theories. If you are developing theory in this way, you will have stated clear hypotheses in advance, and your analytical task will be to measure or match up your data against these.

2   Theory comes last and is developed from or through data generation and analysis. If you are developing theory in this way, you will probably begin the process of analysis whilst data generation is under way, and use a version of theoretical sampling to augment this. You will scrutinize your data so that you can develop explanations which appear to fit them.

3   Theory, data generation and data analysis are developed simultaneously in a dialectical process. If you are developing theory in this way, you will devise a method for moving back and forth between data analysis and the process of explanation or theory construction.

You will undoubtedly be able to match these different possibilities more or less with different research philosophies, although you will also discover that different commentators may match them in different ways (see Blaikie, 1993, Chapters 5 and 6 for a very useful review). For example, the 'theory comes first' view (answer 1) is probably most closely allied with *deductive reasoning*, or what is sometimes called the 'hypothetico-deductive method', whereby theoretical propositions or hypotheses are generated in advance of the research process, and then modified – usually through a process of falsification – by the empirical research. This is often characterized as moving from the general to the particular. The 'theory comes last' view (answer 2) looks much more like *inductive reasoning*, where the researcher will develop theoretical propositions or explanations out of the data, in a process which is commonly seen as moving from the particular to the general. This is probably most famously associated within the qualitative research tradition with Glaser and Strauss's 'grounded theorizing', whereby explanation and theory are fashioned directly from the emerging analysis of the data – using what Glaser and Strauss (1967) call the 'constant comparative method'. However, it is worth pointing out that Glaser and Strauss's approach can also be matched with the third option, where theory, data analysis and data generation are produced dialectically. Blaikie's characterizations of 'abductive reasoning' and 'retroductive reasoning' probably also match answer 3. The former is associated with the interpretive tradition and, in particular, the process of moving between everyday concepts and meanings, lay accounts, and social science explanations. The latter is associated with the realist tradition, and in particular the process whereby the social scientist develops explanatory models of underlying mechanisms which are said to account for empirical observations. The models will include some kind of statement about how – if they are correct – they might operate under different circumstances, and what the empirical manifestations would look like, so that they can in effect be empirically tested.

However, although such associations can be made between different approaches to the timing and logistics of the production and development of theory, and different philosophical traditions in the social sciences, it is worth pointing out that most research strategies probably draw on a combination of these approaches. It is certainly debatable whether 'pure' forms of, for example, inductive, deductive, abductive or retroductive reasoning are ever actually practised. Certainly, the idea that theory can ever come last has been much criticized, since in its most naive form this appears to assume that research can be begun and undertaken in a theoretical vacuum, an assumption which I have criticized earlier. Nevertheless, whether or not pure forms exist, you do need to be clear in general terms about whether the impetus to theorize is going to come first, last, or dialectically, in your research, since as I have suggested this certainly has implications for how you go about sorting and organizing your data, and drawing on them to build your explanations.

- The final version of an answer to these questions leads directly from the previous answer, but instead of asking a question about the role of empirical data *per se* in your theories and explanations, it should focus your attention on how to decide on the role of different 'slices', segments and forms of data. Specifically, it involves asking:

Is this 'slice', segment or form of data illustrative or constitutive of my explanation?

It is important to focus your mind on whether a slice or segment of data is actually integral to, or constitutive of, your explanation, or whether it merely provides an illustration of it. Platt (1988) makes a similar distinction between the 'logical' and 'rhetorical' functions of data.

Imagine, for example, that you have extracted from a set of interview transcripts some quotable chunks of text in relation to a cross-sectional indexing category. The quotations might be, for example, taken from 25 out of 30 transcripts, and might involve interviewees explaining their household division of labour to the interviewer. You might be wishing to construct an explanation of gender relations in the household. You will need to think carefully about how and whether you use these quotations to develop your explanation. First, is this theme itself – the household division of labour – integral to, or constitutive of, the explanation? In other words, does the household division of labour simply illustrate something about household gender relations, or does it produce or epitomize such relations? Did you actually use this slice of data to develop your explanation, or did you develop the explanation and then use this slice of data to illustrate it? Could the explanation have been developed without this slice of data? Or, was the explanation developed on the basis of other data? If so, do the quotations contained within this slice add anything to your explanation? Do they make logical sense when presented simply as quotations, or do they need to be contextualized in some way? Do they simply help to illustrate key points in your explanation, or to make the explanation more immediate and grounded for a potential audience?

Answering these questions will help you to decide whether your slice of data is constitutive or illustrative of your explanation, and you will then need to decide how to use it in presenting and demonstrating your explanation. Is it, for example, relevant to your explanation that quotations of this type were found in 25 out of 30 transcripts – that is, a majority? Is it relevant – it almost certainly is – which transcripts they

were found within, and at what point in the sequence of dialogue, and
so on? The answers to these questions will of course be fairly
meaningless unless you tie them in with your sampling strategy, and the
composition of your sample. For example, the answers will be contingent upon whether your sample is empirically representative of a wider
population, or whether it constitutes a relevant range in relation to a
wider empirical or theoretical universe, and so on (see Chapter 5). Do
you need to *cite* any of the quotations when establishing and presenting
your explanation – can you imagine presenting this part of your
explanation without doing so? What would be the implications of that?
Could you, for example, instead simply state that 25 interviewees said *x*
or *y* about their division of household labour without directly quoting
any of them? If you decide you do need to cite some of the quotations,
on what basis are you going to decide which to choose? You must make
clear what is the strategic rationale for such choices. Are you, for
example, choosing at random because any of the quotations, and the
interviewees and contexts which yielded them, will perform the same
function in the explanation? This is unlikely, and instead you will need
to make selections strategically (again probably in connection with your
sampling strategy). Perhaps most importantly, you will need to *explain
what is the relationship of the quotations or slices of data you have
chosen to cite to those which you have not.* You can express this
relationship numerically (for example, this quotation, made by a man,
is one of 25 similar types generated from 20 women and 5 men, and so
on) and/or qualitatively (this quotation is typical, extreme, a particularly articulate expression of a point, and so on). In practice, you will
probably wish to express the relationship in both numerical and
qualitative terms.

   In thinking about these issues you may find the distinction between
whether or not slices of data are illustrative or constitutive of your
explanations begins to blur or at least overlap. I do not think this
matters, because the purpose of the exercise is to ensure that you are
thinking carefully, every time, about the role you expect slices and
segments of data to perform in your explanations, rather than expecting
them simply to work for you in an unthought-out way. You will need to
do this whether or not you are intending to integrate different forms of
data in your analysis. However, where you are attempting to achieve
this kind of integration, you must think clearly about which parts of the
intellectual puzzle you expect different forms or types of data to
address (see discussion of validity, below; see also Chapter 2; and see
Mason, 1994).

We have begun to move in this section from questions about constructing
explanations, to questions about presenting them to an audience. We are
now ready to confront directly the question of how you go about producing
explanations which are convincing, on the basis of qualitative data analysis.

CONVINCING YOURSELF AND OTHERS

It is not enough simply to be aware of what kind of explanation you are constructing, and to assemble your data in support of it. You will also need to work out how best to ensure that your explanation, and the analysis on which it is based, is *convincing*. This presents you with a twofold task: first, you must convince yourself that you are producing a sound and well founded analysis, and then you must work out how to convince others that this is what you have done. This should involve explaining why *your* explanation, rather than potential alternatives, is the best or most appropriate. You should anticipate that others will not be easy to convince, and it is sensible therefore also to make sure that you yourself are not easily convinced. This will involve putting your analysis to the test, and making sure that it is both systematically and transparently constructed. You need to be able to demonstrate to yourself and others that you proceeded in a rigorous fashion and that you made reasonable and well founded assumptions in the process. Making all of this transparent effectively means that you should be demonstrating to others how you reached your explanation.

I think there are three key elements which you should work your way through in order to produce an explanation which is convincing to yourself and to others. These are well known ways in which social research is conventionally judged, but you will need to work out what they mean for qualitative research in general, and your own project in particular. They are questions of: reliability and accuracy of method; validity of data; and generalizability of analyses. We will consider each in turn.

> How can I demonstrate that my methods are reliable and accurate?

Conventional measures of reliability are more comfortably associated with quantitative research where standardized 'research instruments' are used than they are with qualitative research. So, for example, reliability is sometimes measured by observing the consistency with which the same methods of data 'collection' produce the same results. The logic is that, if you measure the same phenomenon more than once with the same instrument, then you should get the same measurement, just as, for example, three accurate and standardized tape-measures will produce consistent measurements of the same length or piece of cloth. Reliability is therefore being conceptualized in terms of how reliable, accurate and precise the research *tools* or instruments are, and this in turn is being judged by the consistency with which known instruments produce certain 'measurements'. All of this is premised on the assumption that methods of data generation can be conceptualized as tools, and can be standardized, neutral and non-biased. As I argued in Chapters 3 and 4, however, these assumptions are ones with which most qualitative researchers would want to take issue. At the very least, given the non-standardization of many methods for generating qualitative data, a researcher will be unable to perform simple reliability tests of this type because the data they generate will not take the form of a clearly standardized set of measurements. Indeed, it is possible to argue that an obsession with reliability – which may occur precisely because it can apparently be 'measured' – inappropriately overshadows more important questions of validity, resulting in a nonsensical situation where a researcher may be not at all clear about what they are measuring (validity), but can nevertheless claim to be measuring it with a great deal of precision (reliability).

Despite these criticisms of conventional measures of reliability, it is important to emphasize that qualitative researchers of course must be concerned with overall questions of reliability and accuracy in their methods and research practice, albeit in a rather different way. I think this concern should be expressed in terms of ensuring – and demonstrating to others – that your data generation and analysis have been not only appropriate to the research questions, but also thorough, careful, honest and accurate (as distinct from true or correct – terms which many qualitative researchers would, of course, wish to reject). At the very least, this means you must satisfy yourself and others that you have not invented or misrepresented your data, or been careless and slipshod in your recording and analysis of data. In order to convince others, you must provide some sort of account of exactly how you achieved the degree of reliability and accuracy you claim to be providing. The presentation of your analysis must therefore include an explanation of why it is that the audience should believe it to be reliable and accurate.

The next question involves judging the validity of your research.

> How can I demonstrate that my analysis is valid?

Judgements of validity are, in effect, judgements about whether you are 'measuring', or explaining, what you claim to be measuring or explaining. They therefore concern your conceptual and ontological clarity, and the success with which you have translated these into a meaningful and relevant epistemology. If you claim you are studying, for example, the effects of a specified social policy, can you demonstrate that your explanation does concern the effects of that policy, rather than perhaps a wider set of influences and social changes, or a completely different set of policies? If you claim you are studying everyday views or attitudes about national government, can you demonstrate that you are tapping into views or attitudes, rather than behaviours, or accounts? Can you show that these are everyday views, rather than views initiated by a specific context such as a political event which occurred the day before, or indeed the fact of your own research and the impact of your interest on those whom you are researching? Can you be sure that you are getting at views of national government, rather than, for example, local government, or a particular political figure? These questions of validity involve ontological and conceptual clarity in the sense that you will need to be clear about what it is you mean by, for example, everyday views or attitudes, and they also involve relevant epistemology in that you will need to demonstrate that your research strategy has appropriately honed in on these elements.

Given the concerns about the appropriateness of measures of reliability of method, qualitative researchers tend to prefer to focus their interest and efforts on what they see as the more sophisticated and meaningful concept of validity. You should think about how to demonstrate the validity of your method and analysis in at least two ways.

- *Validity of data generation methods* is the first of these. This involves asking what it is that you think your data sources and generation methods can potentially tell you, and how well they can do this. You will of course already have engaged with these questions in planning and designing your research, and in thinking through the logic of each of your chosen data generation methods. You can think about the validity of your methods in both broad and detailed ways.

   Broadly, you will be asking how well matched is the logic of the method to the kinds of research questions you are asking, and the kind of social explanation you are intending to develop. So, for example, if you want to explain the process of learning and individual development in children, you will already have decided how you think such a process can potentially be explained (as distinct from what the content of the explanation is). As a qualitative researcher, you are probably more likely to pursue an explanation constructed from a detailed and close-up analysis of what you see as the mechanics of this process, perhaps by developing longitudinal case studies of individual children's experiences, lives, biographies, their own interpretive understandings of learning and development, and so on. An alternative approach might be to trace empirical 'indicators' of learning and development, by perhaps taking 'snapshots' of the performance of large numbers of children in school examinations and relating these to variables like age, gender, social class, and so on. You will have developed your own views on which methodological approach is the more valid in relation to your own research questions, and which kinds of explanations can account for which kinds of social phenomena. In the process of data analysis and the presentation of your explanation to others, you should therefore revisit those difficult questions which you asked yourself about linking research questions, methodology and methods, when you were designing your research. When it comes to convincing others, you must show how you reached decisions on these issues, and by what logic you are connecting your chosen methods with your intellectual puzzle and research questions.

Detailed as opposed to broad ways of thinking about validity in relation to your data generation methods involve a more particular application of the same kind of logic. So, instead of demonstrating how and why your methodological strategy is a valid way to pursue your research questions, these involve showing how particular methods, aspects of methods, or data sources, do this. There is a blurring of the distinction between validity and reliability here, since you will be reflecting on the quality of your methods in relation to your research questions, and on how well they produce relevant data which can be used in constructing your explanation. So, for example, if you are conducting interviews, or analysing documents, you will need to reflect not only on how effectively interviewing or documentary analysis *as strategies* can illuminate the concepts in which you are interested, but also on the capacity of *this* interviewee or document, or *this* set of questions, or *this* interaction, to do so. You might ask, for example, how authentic, accurate or relevant is a particular document in relation to what you want to know. You may wish to regard data generated from some interviews as more valid in relation to your research questions than those generated from others. If so, you must figure out for yourself, and be able to demonstrate to others, how you are able to make such judgements. Do you, for example, think that a particular interviewee is deceiving you? Is it that you were unable to understand or communicate effectively with a particular interviewee? Do you think that one interviewee is better placed than another to account for whatever it is that you are interested in? Do you think that something to do with the social dynamics of the interview interaction has had a specific influence on validity? Of course, as discussed in Chapter 3, most qualitative researchers see the very fluidity and flexibility of methods such as semi-structured interviewing as enhancing validity, and criticize the rigidity and standardization of structured questionnaires by contrast for lack of sensitivity to validity in favour of an excessive concern with reliability and ease of quantification in analysis. But if this is the case, you must explain how and why you reach that conclusion, if you are to convince others.

I think that a general dictum that you should explain how *you* came to the conclusion that your methods were valid is a better way to demonstrate validity to others than some of the more specific methods which are sometimes recommended. In particular, I am thinking of the technique of 'triangulation of method' here (see Denzin, 1989, Chapter 10). In its broadest sense, triangulation refers to the use of a combination of methods to explore one set of research questions, and I have no argument with that idea. Indeed, in Chapter 2 I advocated the careful and considered inclusion of multiple methods in research designs. However, at its worst, the logic of triangulation says that you can use different methods, or data sources, to investigate the same phenomena, and that in the process you can judge the efficacy or validity of the different methods and sources by comparing the products. The idea is that, if you measure the same phenomenon from different angles or positions, you will get an accurate reading or measurement of it. This is problematic because, as I have consistently argued throughout the book, different methods and data sources are likely to throw light onto different social or ontological phenomena or research questions (or to provide different versions or 'levels' of answer). Furthermore, it implies a view of the social world which says that there is one, objective, and knowable social reality, and all that social researchers have to do is to work out which are the most appropriate triangulation points to measure it by – a view with which many researchers in the qualitative tradition would of course take issue. You are highly unlikely, therefore, to be able straightforwardly to use the 'products' of different methods or sources to corroborate (or otherwise) each other. If you are expecting to use triangulation in this sense, you are likely to become very confused about matters of validity, because you will have more than one data set which seem inexplicably to be pointing in different directions. At its best, I think the concept of triangulation – conceived as multiple methods – encourages the researcher to approach their research questions from different angles, and to explore their intellectual puzzles in a rounded and multi-faceted way. This does enhance validity, in the sense that it suggests that social phenomena are a little more than one-dimensional, and that your study has accordingly managed to grasp more than one of those dimensions. However, the use of the term 'triangulation' for this best case scenario is probably misleading since it is commonly under-stood to be a technique for checking out one method against another. The general message, then, is that you should not expect the use of multiple methods or triangulation to provide an easy or well trodden route to the demonstration of validity of method.

- *Validity of interpretation* is the second way in which you should think about validity. This involves asking how valid is your data analysis, and the interpretation on which it is based. It is of course dependent upon validity of method, since your interpretation cannot be valid unless your methods and sources have enabled you at least to get at the concepts you say you are getting at. However, it goes further than this in that it directs attention to the quality and rigour with which you have interpreted and analysed your data in relation to your intellectual puzzle. What makes you think that your analysis is a valid one? Why should your audience accept your interpretation over any alternatives? Why should they believe that you have not misinterpreted your data?

  In my experience, many researchers encounter crises of confidence about the validity of their own interpretations. Given that qualitative researchers are usually wanting to make interpretive readings of their data, there sometimes comes a point when they find themselves asking, 'Have I simply made this interpretation up? Have I invented it?' You may be especially vulnerable to this feeling if you have, along with many other qualitative researchers, rejected the notion of one objective and true reality which can simply be 'discovered' with rigorous and careful research instruments. The challenge in this case is how to demonstrate that your interpretation is indeed valid, without resorting to claims to ultimate truth and objectivity which you are likely to see as emanating from a discourse you have rejected.

In my view, validity of interpretation in any form of qualitative research is contingent upon the 'end product' including a demonstration of how that interpretation was reached. This means that you should be able to, and be prepared to, trace the route by which you came to your interpretation. You must spell out on what basis you have felt able to, for example, interpret a piece of dialogue from an interview, or a set of observations from a particular setting, or a section of a document, as reflecting upon a particular ontological concept or set of issues. Furthermore, you must explain how you have woven sections of data together (for example, you might have done this cross-sectionally by theme, or holistically by 'case') to produce an interpretation of how specific instances in your data set can be read together as saying something about, for example, social processes. The basic principle here is that you are never taking it as self-evident that a particular interpretation can be made of your data but instead that you are continually and assiduously charting and justifying the steps through which your interpretations were made. If you do this effectively, it should enable you to show both that you have understood and engaged with your own position, or standpoint, or analytical lens, in a *reflexive* sense, and also that you have tried to read your data from alternative interpretive perspectives. The validity of your interpretation will be strengthened both if you can give some sense of how your standpoint or analytical lens feeds into your interpretation, and also if you can show why the other interpretive perspectives which you have considered are less compelling than your own.

I do not think that all of this implies that the qualitative researcher is compelled to write an enormous treatise on their methodology to accompany every publication or presentation of their analyses. It certainly means that methods and methodology must be explained and justified, but the most effective way to do this is to get into the habit of taking nothing for granted about, for example, the transparency to an audience of the logic of your methodological choices or analytical decisions and practices. This means remembering habitually to explain such logic – although you may do this in more depth for some purposes than others – rather than simply presenting your interpretations.

The recommendation that you make transparent how it is that you got to your interpretations, just as I argued that you should trace the logic whereby you made certain methodological choices, runs counter to the idea that there can be 'quick-fix' solutions to the dilemma of validity of interpretation. I want to illustrate this by briefly considering two examples of techniques for enhancing or demonstrating validity of interpretation which can be criticized for failing to take on board the complexity of the issues. The first involves claiming that you have a particular 'standpoint' which grants you epistemological privilege, and the second involves checking the validity of your interpretation with people whom you see as having this kind of epistemological privilege – a procedure sometimes called 'respondent validation'.

The standpoint position has received much critical discussion and scrutiny in feminist research and epistemology (see especially Haraway, 1988; Harding, 1986; Holland and Ramazanoglu, 1994; Maynard, 1994; Rose, 1994; Smith, 1988; Stanley and Wise, 1993), but has also been influential in other areas such as disability or emancipatory research (see especially Oliver, 1992). The argument is one which suggests that epistemological privilege is granted by one's social location and experience, particularly in relation to oppression (for example, based on gender, or based on disability), and in relation to the focus of the research. The crude position is, therefore, that women are best placed as researchers to understand women's oppression, as are disabled people to understand oppression based on disability. I do not wish to take issue with the idea that one's personal experiences are relevant to, and useful in, research, and indeed the notion of reflexivity of course is built on recognition of the salience of such experiences through the process of turning one's analytical lens on oneself. However, the problem lies in the suggestion that the experience of a form of oppression by an individual researcher unquestionably gives that researcher insider knowledge of such oppression as it is experienced by everyone else. Much of the feminist critical debate about standpoint epistemologies has focused on the misleading impression this gives of, for example, the unity and sameness of women's experiences. But the problem is exacerbated in the extent to which such claims to epistemological privilege are used to support validity claims, by effectively placing the researcher and their judgement beyond question or critical scrutiny. My point really is this: standpoint positions cannot be unequivocally regarded as granting epistemological privilege to such an extent that the researcher has no need to demonstrate the validity of their interpretations in any other way. They are, therefore, not the quick-fix of interpretive validity.

The second example seems, on the face of it, to be less controversial, since it involves arguing that others – not you yourself as researcher – have epistemological privilege. The classic example of this is the practice of presenting research 'subjects' such as interviewees, or people involved in settings which were observed, with extracts of your analysis and interpretation. The idea that this can be used to support validity is based on the notion that research subjects are in a position to judge and confirm (or otherwise) the validity of the interpretations the researcher has made. However, this too is problematic. As Skeggs has noted, the most common response from her research subjects to this practice was 'Can't understand a bloody word it says' (1994: 86), and of course this is more than a practical problem. The issue really is this: just as I have argued that a single researcher cannot unequivocally claim epistemological privilege simply because they belong to a specifically defined social group, or occupy a specific social location, so too we cannot assume that a single research subject (or even a group of research subjects) unequivocally possesses such privilege. Indeed, given that qualitative researchers are likely to be trading in social science interpretations, based on social science conventions, there is no reason to suppose that research subjects who are unfamiliar with these will have either interest in them, or knowledge about how they operate. I am not arguing that researchers should never share their research in some way with their research subjects. Nor am I denying that it can be useful to check the reliability and accuracy of, for example, interview transcripts with interviewees (although again, where accuracy is disputed, you will need to think about how you will judge whether this is because it is indeed an inaccurate record of the interview which took place, or whether it is based on a *post hoc* rationalization, or on the interviewee's current ideas about what they meant to say in the interview, and so on). Instead, I am pointing out that you cannot expect the practice of asking research subjects to check your *interpretations* to be a quick-fix to the problem of interpretive validity. If you think they do have epistemological privilege enabling them to do this, just as if you think you yourself have epistemological privilege based on a standpoint position, then you will need to demonstrate how and why they (and you) have come to hold that privilege. You cannot assume that such a position is beyond question.

Validity of method and of interpretation therefore must be demonstrated through a careful retracing and reconstruction of the route by which you think you reached them, and there are no easy answers or shortcuts in this process. Let us now turn to the third and final set of issues which you will need to work your way through in the process of convincing yourself, and convincing others, of the value of your explanation. These concern the question of the generalizability of your analyses.

> What kinds of generalizations or wider claims can I make on the basis of my analysis and explanation?

This question will encourage you to think about the wider resonance of your research. If you have conducted a study, for example, of one political organization, or of 30 people's illegal activities, or of the process of change in three educational institutions, you will need to think carefully about the extent to which your explanations have any wider resonance outside of those specific contexts.

It is useful to think about generalization in two ways: empirical generalization and theoretical generalization. The first is based on a logic whereby you are able to make generalizations from an analysis of one empirical population (say, your sample) to another, wider, population (say, all adults in Britain), on the basis that your study population was statistically representative of that wider population. We discussed the logic of this kind of sampling in Chapter 5, and pointed out there that this is the least commonly used method in qualitative research. Therefore, most qualitative researchers are unable or unwilling to attempt to generalize their explanations in this way. The second type of generalization – theoretical generalization – is likely to be more productive. However, it does not represent one uniform method of generalizing, but instead encompasses a range of strategies based on differing logics, some of which look more obviously 'theoretical' than others. Your first task will be to work out what kinds of theoretical generalizations can be made – and on what basis – in the context of your specific research project. Let us consider some of the possibilities, beginning with the least 'theoretical'.

- You may wish to argue that, although you have not based your analysis on data derived from a sample which is representative of a wider population, and you are therefore not attempting to make empirical generalizations, nevertheless you have no reason to assume that your sample and therefore your analysis are atypical. This is, of course, a rather weak way to attempt to generalize, since you are unlikely to be able to make any stronger claims about the typicality of your sample and analysis, unless your sampling strategy actively supports them (see Chapter 5). It is a mode of generalizing which has more in common with an empirical than a theoretical logic. Having *no reason to suspect atypicality* is therefore usually viewed as an adjunct to stronger ways of generalizing theoretically, and ways which are more appropriate to qualitative research. You might therefore compare the characteristics of your sample of interviewees, of settings, of documents, of photographs, or whatever, to the characteristics of the wider population from which they were drawn, in order to be able to support a 'no reason to suspect atypicality' claim, or indeed to chart some of the dimensions on which your sample is indeed atypical. But you are unlikely to view this as the only basis on which you can argue your research has a wider resonance.

- You may produce an analysis for example of processes in a specified setting which demonstrate at the very least that it is possible for such processes to work in a specified way. Your explanation of how and why these processes worked in this way in this setting may be based on a detailed and holistic analysis of the setting, derived from a range of data sources and methods. On this basis – that is, establishing what is possible (that is, 'this happened therefore it can happen'), and having an explanation of how and why it happened in this setting (that is, 'these seemed to be the key explanatory factors and elements in the process in this setting') – you may try to widen the resonance of your explanation by asking questions about the *lessons for other settings*. This form of generalization is therefore based on the idea that you can use your detailed and holistic explanation of one setting, or set of processes, to frame relevant questions about others. Your ability to go further, and to draw conclusions about those other settings and processes, will of course be limited by the extent of their similarity or difference, on the key dimensions as you have defined them, to the first setting.

- You may wish to argue that you have produced an explanation of *an extreme or pivotal case, or set of processes*, and you might have done this in tandem with your sampling strategy. You might, therefore, argue that you are able to explain a set of issues or processes which are, perhaps, central to a developing body of theory, or which involve pivotal elements of social and political change, or what Schofield calls cases at the 'leading edge of change' (1993: 214), or which are extreme or unusual in other ways which are both definable, and relevant to a wider body of theory, knowledge or existence. In each of these examples, you will be seeking to generalize, or to claim a wider resonance, following a slightly different logic, but the common thread is that your explanation throws light on processes or issues which are pivotal or central to some wider body of explanation or knowledge.

- Whatever else you do, you should make some claims for the wider resonance or generalizability of your explanations which are based on *the rigour of your analysis*. It should go without saying that you must be able to demonstrate reliability or accuracy of method, and validity of both method and interpretation, if you are going to have anything meaningful to generalize. Taking these as a starting point, there are further ways in which you can nevertheless increase the generalizability of your analyses and explanations. For example, you may wish to argue that you have built *strategic comparisons* into your research practice and your analysis. Strategic comparisons will be those which enable you to test and develop theoretical and explanatory propositions, and they can be incorporated via your sampling strategy (see Chapter 5), and your analytical practice. Thus, you may choose to include sampling units in your study which you think express key dimensions of your intellectual puzzle, or interesting possibilities which you want to 'test out' in some way. You are therefore defining the significance of your sampling units in theoretical (not empirical) terms, and are thinking about what can usefully be compared with what in order to test out and advance your explanatory thinking. The same principles can guide your analytical practice, whether you are making comparisons between sampling units, people, documents, themes, instances, experiences, processes, cross-sectional indexing categories, holistic elements, or whatever. Basically, you will be seeking to make comparisons which can contribute more to your explanation than a simple statement of sameness or difference.

You may wish to take this further in an explicit attempt to *test out your developing explanation* by trying out alternative explanations, and in particular by looking for negative instances. Again, this is a strategy which can be employed via both your sampling strategy and your analytical practice. I emphasized in Chapter 5 that, if you are using some form of theoretical sampling, then you should ensure that you select sampling units not only in a way which supports your own developing explanation of your intellectual puzzle, but also in a way which allows you to put it to the test. Similarly, in your analytical practice, you can ensure that you make comparisons, and ask questions of your data set, in such a way as to try not only to build up your explanation, but to seek and try out alternative explanations. The role of negative instances is that you would look for examples, themes, cases, or whatever, which run counter to the explanation which you are developing. These might take the form of situations which you would least expect to see, if your explanation were adequate. Although this is a technique which has been developed as part of a broader approach called 'analytic induction' (see Denzin, 1989), you do not have to take on board all the elements of that approach in order to employ it usefully. In particular, many researchers using analytic induction have been seeking to generate explanations from which they wish to claim they can derive universal laws, yet both that goal, and this way of achieving it, have been roundly criticized (see especially Hammersley, 1992). However, if you are able to demonstrate not only that you developed an explanation of your intellectual puzzle, but that you put it to the test in this way, then the rigour of your analysis, and the potential for saying it has a wider theoretical resonance, are much increased.

You will also wish to demonstrate the rigour of your analysis by showing that you have *used aggregation, numbers and counting in a meaningful fashion*. To begin with, this means making sure that you have not tried to make inappropriate empirical generalizations which cannot be supported by your sampling strategy or research practice. So, if your sample is not empirically representative of a wider population, you must not make claims which suggest that it is. Similarly, as argued in Chapter 6, you should not treat cross-sectional indexing categories as though they are variables (unless you have adopted a practice which is consistent with this) which can be fed into a quantitative form of variable analysis. Many of the computer packages for analysing qualitative data will tempt you to do this, and will produce statistical data on the content and shape of your indexing categories (such as the percentage of material categorized by each one). This may be useful, but the fact that a cross-sectional indexing category such as 'inheritance strategies' applies to 40% of the text in a given document or interview transcript is not in itself very interesting or significant. You will need to establish a great many other things about the document or interview in order to make any sense of this information, and your analytical activities may be more usefully spent in making strategic comparisons between different versions of inheritance strategies in the context of different biographies or life stories. Similarly, counting up or aggregating analytical units within your data set makes little sense on its own unless the units are equivalent, which frequently they are not in qualitative analysis. So, for example, experiences, instances, interactions, expressions of belief, accounts, and so on, are not readily aggregated without a great deal of qualification and contextualization. Therefore, it is very important that numbers, aggregation and quantification, are used in ways which are sensitive to the type and form of data, and to the context of their production, and in ways which are complementary to the other methods of achieving theoretical generalizability. Used in such a way, these strategies can indeed augment the generalizability of your explanations. The fact that 30 of your 40 interviewees had specific sets of experiences might indeed have a wider resonance, and you will have a clearer understanding of what that resonance is if you can establish that you selected them on the basis that they were particularly *un*likely to have these experiences, or if your interview practice made it rather *un*likely that such experiences would get mentioned at all. In other words, the numbers make sense only in the wider context of your research strategy and practice (see Mason, 1994).

These different ways of generalizing, or claiming a wider resonance, for qualitative research, must clearly be linked with other aspects of your research design and practice if they are to be effective, and it is worth asking yourself questions about what kinds of links you can and should be making, as follows.

What kinds of generalizations do my *research questions* imply?

We saw earlier that explanations can do a number of things: for example they can compare, develop and trace, describe, predict and theorize. Your research questions will imply not only certain kinds of explanation, but also certain kinds of generalization, and it is of course important to ensure that your research design and practice actually support these. This is part of the art of research design, and in particular of the linking of research questions, methodologies and methods (see Chapter 2). So, for example, you might have asked a question which implies an empirical generalization to a wider, specified, population, such as 'do people in France believe that the threat of nuclear war is over?' Or you might have asked a question which implies a theoretical generalization, such as 'how has the process of educational change evolved?' You probably will, nevertheless, have expressed some empirical parameters in relation to your proposed theoretical generalizations, and you might also have been fairly specific about what kinds of theoretical generalizations you would be able to make. So, for example, we could rephrase the last question as 'how has the process of educational change evolved in Toytown University since the early 1980s?' and 'what lessons can we learn from this for other British universities?' You must, therefore, make clear links between the kinds of questions you ask, the forms of generalization they imply, and your research and analytical practice.

> What kinds of generalizations does
> my *sampling strategy* support?

We discussed this in some detail in Chapter 5, and some of the key forms of theoretical generalization outlined above are clearly contingent on having been sampled in certain ways, and understanding the implications of your sampling strategy. In most cases, empirical generalizations cannot be supported by qualitative sampling strategies, but theoretical generalizations clearly are supported by theoretical and strategic or purposive sampling. Your sampling strategy may provide the key to how you should understand numerical patterns in your data, as well as what significance you should grant to the 'discovery' of what you think are pivotal cases or examples. It can aid the process of theory development and testing. In general, your sampling strategy should provide an important backdrop against which you 'read' and interpret your data (see Platt, 1988). This remains the case even where, possibly for pragmatic reasons, you think you have been unable to be very strategic about sampling. Nevertheless, understanding your own strategy, and in particular the relationship you have established between your sample and a broader empirical or theoretical universe, is a vital part of the analytical endeavour.

> What kinds of generalizations do *my*
> *methods of sorting and organizing*
> *data* support?

We asked this question the other way round in the previous chapter. Basically, cross-sectional indexing and categorical analysis on the one hand, and holistic analysis on the other, potentially support different analytical logics. They imply that you will build up your explanations in certain ways, and therefore they influence the claims to generalizability which you will be able to make. In practice, as I pointed out, many qualitative researchers use both strategies. Cross-sectional analysis implies that you are making comparisons across the whole of your data set, around certain specified themes. This form of analysis therefore does not insist upon, although it can certainly tolerate, a strategic approach to comparison. In other words, the focus of the activity is in comparing everything on the basis of specified themes, rather than selecting specific comparisons in order to test out developing explanations. Holistic analysis more obviously fits the latter form of comparison although, again, it does not insist upon it. You will need to think carefully about which form of analysis (or whether both together) would provide the better support for your developing explanation. This contributes to the generalizability of your explanation by improving the rigour of your analysis.

Generalization is not easy to achieve in qualitative research – or indeed in any research. It requires that you think carefully, and act strategically, throughout the whole research process, not just at the end when you are 'writing up'. You will need to be aware of what kinds of explanations you are attempting to construct, as discussed in the first part of this chapter. This means knowing what your explanation is doing (for example, comparing, developing and tracing, and so on), and knowing what is its relationship to the production of theory (for example, at what point theory comes in the analytical process, and also what type of theory – universal laws, underlying mechanisms, interpretive understandings – you are intending to contribute towards). You will need to have framed a research project, and engaged in a research practice, which allow you to do these things. You will need to ensure that your methods are reliable and accurate, and that your analysis is valid. And finally, you will need to be clear about what kinds of generalizations you want to, and are able to, make, and to understand fully how these are supported by all these other elements of your research design and practice. All of this needs to be done in order that you can convince *yourself* that you are making reasonable and well supported generalizations. In order to convince *others*, you need to make visible these strategic and logical elements in your route from designing and conducting your research, to claiming it has this or that wider resonance. Again, as with demonstrating validity to others, I do not think this has to involve you in producing a massive treatise on your methodology, but instead you must get into the habit of supporting each claim you make with the relevant linking material. Thus, if a claim to generalizability is based upon an element of your sampling strategy, or on a particular set of strategic comparisons you made in your analytical practice, or on a search for negative instances which produced none, then you must spell this out when you make the claim. Indeed, in this sense a separate and lengthy treatise on your methodology would be unhelpful, since what is really required is a *contextual* grounding of generalizability claims in the strategies which produced them. In other words, you need to get used to spelling out in what you write or present to others not only what your claims are, but what are your grounds for making them, just as you might if you were making the case for the prosecution or defence in a court of law.

ETHICS AND POLITICS IN ANALYSING AND PRESENTING QUALITATIVE DATA

Finally, you will need to consider the ethics and politics of your arguments, analyses, and explanations, and of the way you are presenting them to a wider audience. This involves asking the familiar questions, raised earlier, about the ongoing ethics of your research practice, but addressing yourself to the specific issues raised by qualitative analysis and data presentation. I do not intend to try to anticipate all of the ethical and political dilemmas which you might face, and indeed there are some very useful discussions of these existing in the literature (see especially Finch, 1984; Hammersley, 1995; Homan, 1991, Chapters 6 and 7; Miles and Huberman, 1994, Chapter 11). Instead, I am selecting a few key issues which apply in particularly sharp form to the analysis and presentation of qualitative data.

> Have I honoured my commitments
> about confidentiality and privacy?
> Have I acted in the spirit of the
> informed consent which I received?

This involves revisiting the question of informed consent and asking yourself whether you do actually have the informed consent of research subjects to analyse data gained from them in the way you have, to make connections and construct explanations in the way you have, and to present in some kind of public way data which are sufficiently contextualized for judgements about reliability, validity and generalizability to be made. It is precisely because qualitative data are not entirely reducible to numbers and charts, but are often based on holistic analyses and presentations of what may be personal, identifiable and idiosyncratic material, that questions of confidentiality and anonymity are raised in particularly sharp form. You should bear in mind the arguments of researchers such as Finch (1984) that qualitative methods – in her case, interviewing – promote a high degree of trust amongst research subjects, which in turn gives us a special responsibility to ensure that we do not abuse that trust by reneging on commitments, acting deceitfully, or producing explanations which may damage the interests of those subjects. The use of visual data, especially literal images like photographs, can make confidentiality impossible to maintain. You will need to make decisions, at this stage, about whether your analytical and presentational practices do allow you to honour your commitments (and I argued earlier that you should not see your commitments in minimalist terms), or whether you will have to jettison some of your data. You should not let yourself off the hook with platitudes like 'it will only be published in an academic journal so my research subjects will probably never see it'. If your research is entering the public domain in any sense whatsoever, and it almost certainly is, then you cannot assume that only those people whom you want to see it will see it.

> Have I fulfilled my responsibility to produce good quality research?

I am taking it as given that researchers do have a responsibility to produce good quality research (see Miles and Huberman, 1994, and especially their discussion of 'competence boundaries' on p. 291). This can be seen as a responsibility to yourself, your research subjects, your funders or sponsors, your institution and colleagues, your profession, the advancement of knowledge in general, and so on. It means that all the earlier questions about reliability and accuracy, validity, and generalizability, are not only intellectual issues, but also cast in an ethical and political hue. So, for example, you will need to put your ethical and political hats on to ask 'have I produced a careful and well founded analysis?', 'have I made any false or inappropriate generalizations?'

> Have I used my research, and my explanations, effectively?

Different researchers will have a different sense of responsibility to use their research to contribute to some wider body of debate or practice, and this relates to the question posed in Chapter 2: 'What is the purpose of my research? What am I doing it for?' Some research is seen as highly political, or 'emancipatory', and if this applies to you then you will have been grappling throughout the research process with questions about how to use it most effectively (see Finch, 1986, for an excellent discussion of the use of qualitative research in social and educational policy). However, I agree with Hammersley that all qualitative research, whether or not it is overtly political or emancipatory, should be 'relevant to some legitimate public concern' (1992: 68). At the very least, if you are to use your research effectively, you will need to ensure that:

- you do try to make some forms of generalization
- you do not make inappropriate or false generalizations
- your generalizations are framed in such a way that they feed into wider sets of issues or questions, or help to initiate debate about issues and questions which you see as 'legitimate public concerns'.

> Do I have a responsibility to anticipate how others might use my research and explanations?

This issue is often discussed in the context of protecting the rights or interests of your research subjects: do you have a responsibility to anticipate how others might use your research, and even how they might misappropriate it, or misinterpret it? If you accept the arguments of writers like Finch (1984) that qualitative researchers have a special responsibility because of the high degree of trust generated between researcher and research subject through the use of some qualitative methods, then your answer must be yes, you do have this responsibility. At the very least, you will have to think carefully about, and work out your stance on, the interests of those directly and indirectly involved in your research. Of course this might apply not only to your research subjects, but to other groups or interests to which you (or others – appropriately or inappropriately) might generalize your arguments. It will also apply to other 'stakeholders' in the research process, such as your funders or sponsors, your institution, your colleagues, your profession, and so on.

> In general, am I clear about both my rights, and my responsibilities, in respect of my data, my analysis and my explanations?

I have encouraged you throughout to think carefully about your ethical and political responsibilities, but you should also, of course, think about your rights. You will need to be clear about who owns the data you have generated, and what rights the owners have over them. Whilst legal issues about ownership are, to an extent, enshrined in for example copyright and patenting laws, and codes of practice relating to intellectual property, there are many grey areas where the issues are less than clear cut. You must explore what your rights and responsibilities seem to be, not just for your own sake but again for the sake of others who have interests in the research.

For example, are you legally in a position to make the kinds of guarantees about confidentiality which you would like to make to your research subjects? Can you guarantee privacy and confidentiality in relation to the use of a set of documents?

There is, of course, no ethical or political blueprint to guide you through your analytical practice. As always, you will need to make decisions which are difficult, and where there is not one clear ethical course of action. You may be balancing competing interests, all of which you see as legitimate. You will therefore have to make decisions based on compromise and context but these must, of course, come from a considered ethical position (as I argued in Chapter 2).

CONCLUSION

We have covered some difficult ground in this chapter. The analysis of qualitative data is not an easy task, and the construction of explanations needs to be done with rigour, with care, and with a great deal of intellectual and strategic thinking. Until recently, almost all of the published literature on qualitative research focused on methods for generating data, and although there are now some very useful contributions about how you might analyse such data and construct explanations and theories on their basis (see 'further reading' below and in Chapter 6), the territory is still rather sparsely charted.

I have tried to emphasize throughout the chapter that there are different types of social explanation, and different ways of supporting them, even within what some commentators might like to see as a unified qualitative tradition. Ultimately, what you do must depend upon the way you have framed your research questions, the philosophical and methodological posture which they encapsulate, the way you have designed your project to support these, and the realities of the research process which you have pursued.

FURTHER READING

Atkinson, P. (1992) *Understanding Ethnographic Texts*, London: Sage

Blaikie, N. (1993) *Approaches to Social Enquiry*, Cambridge: Polity (especially Chapters 5 and 6)

Bryman, A. and Burgess, R.G. (eds) (1994) *Analyzing Qualitative Data*, London: Routledge

Finch, J. (1986) *Research and Policy: the Uses of Qualitative Methods in Social and Educational Research*, London: Falmer

Hammersley, M. (1992) *What's Wrong with Ethnography?*, London: Routledge

Henwood, K.L. and Pidgeon, N.F. (1992) 'Qualitative Research and Psychological Theorizing' *British Journal of Psychology*, vol. 83, pp. 97–111

Holland, J. and Ramazanoglu, C. (1994) 'Coming to Conclusions: Power and Interpretation in Researching Young Women's Sexuality' in M. Maynard and J. Purvis (eds) *Researching*

Women's Lives from a Feminist Perspective, London: Taylor and Francis (a useful discussion of issues of interpretation and standpoints in feminist research)

Homan, R. (1991) *The Ethics of Social Research*, London: Longman (Chapters 6 and 7)

Hughes, J. (1990) *The Philosophy of Social Research*, 2nd edn, London: Longman

Miles, M.B. and Huberman, A.M. (1994) *Qualitative Data Analysis: an Expanded Sourcebook*, 2nd edn, London: Sage (Chapters 10, 11 and 12)

Platt, J. (1988) 'What Can Case Studies Do?' in R.G. Burgess (ed.) *Studies in Qualitative Methodology*, vol. 1, JAI Press, pp. 1–23.

Schofield, J.W. (1993) 'Increasing the Generalizability of Qualitative Research' in M. Hammersley (ed.) *Social Research: Philosophy, Politics and Practice*, London: Sage

Silverman, D. (1993) *Interpreting Qualitative Data: Methods for Analyzing Talk, Text and Interaction*, London: Sage

8

CONCLUSION: THE QUALITATIVE RESEARCH PRACTITIONER

Each of the chapters in this book has examined a more or less discrete element in the qualitative research process, and posed a series of difficult questions. Although the elements are largely discrete in an analytical sense, they do not represent clearly cut and distinguishable sequential stages. I have tried to emphasize in each chapter some of the ways in which the elements are linked – and often concurrent – in practice, at the levels both of thinking and of doing. So, for example, you will need to think through what kind of analysis and explanation you are intending to construct when you are producing your research design and composing your research questions. You will need to sample strategically in order to construct certain types of explanation, and in many cases you will need to have begun the process of data analysis before you finish sampling and data generation. All the time you will be moving – in thought and practice – between intellectual and practical issues. You will be working out the intellectual and practical implications and consequences of all elements in the unfolding research process, and in all the research decisions you make. This emphasis on continuous activity, in both thinking and doing, in my view not only is essential to the production of good qualitative research, but also potentially places qualitative researchers in a rather special position as particular kinds of research practitioners. In this chapter I shall spell out what I mean by this, and examine two areas of contemporary debate on which I think qualitative research practitioners have particularly useful contributions to make: ethics and politics on the one hand, and the integration of different methods on the other.

THE QUALITATIVE RESEARCHER AS A THINKING, REFLEXIVE PRACTITIONER

The idea that qualitative research should be conducted as a reflexive practice is of course not a new one (see for example Hammersley and Atkinson, 1995), and debates about reflexivity have gained significant impetus from feminist ideas about how we should understand the research process and the relative positions of researcher and researched within it (see Maynard and Purvis, 1994; Stanley and Wise, 1993). My continued emphasis on identifying, posing and resolving difficult questions in the research process constitutes a very strong message that we should be reflexive about every decision we take, and that we should not take any decisions without actively recognizing that we are taking them. This casts qualitative researchers in a very active role, not as the followers or even creators of research blueprints, but as *practitioners* who think and act in ways which are situated and contextual but also strategic. There are two elements to this. The first is that in qualitative research traditions there is a long standing emphasis on, and approval of, the idea of reflexivity and, in particular, that the research process should be constructed out of situated and contextual decisions and actions. The second is to do with the lack of blueprints for qualitative research, and also to an extent the less widespread public recognition and approval of qualitative paradigms as compared with the more familiar conventions of quantitative research. Arguably, researchers in more quantitative traditions have greater access to research blueprints, although these are not of course beyond criticism, and they may have less difficulty in getting their work to be publicly recognized as legitimate and convincing. The very absence of clear conventions or blueprints for conducting and analysing qualitative research means to an extent that we are compelled to 'think on our feet' and of course the temptation to do this in an *ad hoc* or haphazard way can be very great. However, in my view, and as I have argued throughout, what we should also do – and especially if we want our work to be taken seriously and perceived as convincing – is to ensure that we make sensible and informed decisions whose products will constitute a meaningful, coherent, intellectually compelling and practicable research *strategy*. This means that we do not produce blueprints in advance of research which we simply follow thereafter, but neither do we fail to plan and instead make *ad hoc* and isolated decisions.

   The imperative to work in this way should not be seen as a disadvantage. I am certainly not trying to suggest that, if only we could develop the blueprints and get public recognition for qualitative paradigms, then we could relax and stop having to be thinking, reflexive practitioners. On the contrary, I think there are great virtues in this kind of practice, and many non-qualitative researchers have a lot to learn from it. (I am not, of course, suggesting that all quantitative researchers are non-thinking and passive blueprint followers.) I want to illustrate this in the rest of this chapter by focusing on two important areas of research debate, and highlighting what I see as some of the specific contributions which qualitative researchers can and have made to them. First, I shall look at questions of ethics and politics in research, and secondly I shall explore some of the issues around integrating different research methods. Both of these sets of issues have been raised at various stages throughout the preceding chapters and I am therefore simply pulling out some key points for discussion here.

ETHICS AND POLITICS IN SOCIAL RESEARCH

The kind of active qualitative research practice which I have described, together with the rather distinctive nature of qualitative data and analysis, raise two important sets of issues for debates about ethics and politics in social research more generally. I shall consider each in turn.

- First, as we have seen, qualitative data tend to be rich and detailed, and the forms of analysis undertaken emphasize the use of this detail in 'holistic' or contextual ways, with only a secondary interest (if any) in turning detail into numbers for statistical manipulation. This means, as we have seen, that the confidentiality and privacy of those who have some personal involvement with the research may be more difficult to maintain than where, for example, data are turned into statistical trends, patterns and correlations. In qualitative research the methods for validating one's analysis tend to emphasize making personal detail and context more rather than less visible to the research audience. Furthermore, we have noted that face-to-face data generating methods such as qualitative interviewing and observation can – and some say should – involve the development of interpersonal relationships between researcher and researched which are characterized by a high degree of trust and confidence (Finch, 1984). As a consequence, a researcher may be treated more as a friend or confidant than a 'detached' professional, and may gain access to data which the researched would share with the former category of person, but not with the latter. Qualitative researchers have to decide what to do with such data, in the knowledge that however friendly they may feel with the researched, and however much they feel the relationship is one of *mutual* trust, they are nevertheless also a professional who is intending to use some of the products of the relationship for another, formal, purpose.

  These are, of course, issues with which qualitative researchers have been grappling for many years and in that sense there is nothing new in what I am saying. But the point I wish to make is that the very act of trying to resolve such difficult dilemmas means that qualitative researchers have had to think in complex and sophisticated ways about confidentiality and privacy, precisely because they do not have the comfort of anonymous statistical analyses based on depersonalized numerical data to 'hide' behind. Qualitative researchers have therefore more wholeheartedly engaged with the idea that informed consent is complex, and may need to be renegotiated throughout the research process as relationships change and develop. Similarly, most qualitative researchers are familiar with the idea that privacy and confidentiality are not only to do with specific disclosures of personal or private data obtained within individually negotiated relationships. Privacy and confidentiality also involve the *interests* both of those who were actually researched, and of others about whom generalizations might be made. In other words, privileged data can be used in ways which have wide ranging impacts, outside of the specific research relationship which generated them (Finch, 1984; Homan, 1991; Miles and Huberman, 1994).

   Whilst qualitative researchers do not necessarily have a monopoly on
these ideas about research ethics, the nature of qualitative data and
analysis mean that they more often *have to* engage with them. Yet, of
course, they are relevant issues in any research, whether or not it is
conceived as falling on one side or another of the so-called qualitative–
quantitative divide. So, for example, more structured ways of generating
data for quantitative analysis, such as structured survey interviews, may
nevertheless feel like the basis of a developing relationship of trust as far
as the interviewee is concerned. Anyone who has tried to conduct a
highly structured and standardized interview will know that interviewee
and interviewer often end up 'chatting round the edges' of the structure.
In this context, the ethics of turning what might be, for example, rich,
detailed and complex life experiences into superficial and static variables
and codes for statistical manipulation can seem just as suspect as using
'too much' of the personal data which was given in trust. And of course
political questions about whose interests are served or damaged by the
overall analysis and use of the research apply with equal resonance to an
analysis based on statistical manipulation as one based on holistic qualitative analysis.

- Secondly, the active and self-questioning qualitative research practice
  which I have advocated means, in general, that qualitative researchers
  will not and cannot be satisfied with standardized or codified answers to
  ethical and political dilemmas. As we saw in Chapter 2, whilst it is
  important to think carefully about one's ethical and political strategy at
  the beginning of the research process, it is nevertheless not possible to
  take all of one's ethical and political decisions once and for all at the start
  and then simply stick to them. This is because ethical and political issues
  arise or take shape contextually throughout the research process, and
  need to be dealt with in ways which are informed and situated rather than
  formal and abstract. I have emphasized throughout that qualitative
  researchers need to develop an ethical and politically aware *practice*,
  based on such contextualized decisions about specific ethical and political dilemmas and issues. It has therefore never been easy for qualitative
  researchers simply to 'follow' ethical codes of conduct (where they
  exist). Such codes or guidelines are usually, of necessity, written in
  formal and abstract terms and focused on 'big' issues such as the use of
  covert or deceptive methods of data generation, or the outright exploitation of or damage to research subjects, and so on. Whilst such codes
  and guidelines are clearly important in establishing a minimal baseline of
  ethical conduct (for example within a social science discipline, or a
  profession, or a research institution), they usually give little guidance
  about how to develop an ethical and politically aware *practice*, or how to
  deal with more 'everyday' ethical and political matters. It is in this
  context that the qualitative researcher, acting as a thinking, reflexive
  practitioner who is constantly asking 'difficult questions' about how

ethics and politics work in practice, has a great deal to contribute to our handling of these matters in social science research.

There is, of course, a lot more that could be said about ethics and politics in research, but these two points represent major contributions which qualitative researchers, acting as thinking, reflexive practitioners, are particularly well placed to make to contemporary debates.

INTEGRATING DIFFERENT RESEARCH METHODS

The second set of issues which I want to highlight concerns the integration of different research methods. I have emphasized throughout that this is not a simple matter, whether or not you think you are integrating methods across some qualitative–quantitative divide, or merely using more than one qualitative method. Indeed, whilst I do not wish to get overly entangled in debates about whether or not there really is such a thing as a divide between quantitative and qualitative methods (Brannen, 1992; Hammersley, 1992), I think it is worth arguing that such a division is decidedly *un*helpful if it is used to suggest either that the integrating of methods across the divide is impossible, or that integration within each broad paradigm is unproblematic. In my view, neither of these assertions is correct. Certainly, integrating methods of data generation which are standardized and structured with those which are not, and integrating modes of analysis which are holistic and processual with those which are cross-sectional and circumstantial, raise difficult issues technically and epistemologically. But these issues are not unique to qualitative–quantitative integration. Qualitative researchers who adopt the practice of asking themselves difficult questions throughout the research process will become accustomed to reflecting on epistemological questions about what count as data and evidence, and about how explanations can be constructed, as well as ontological questions about what constitutes the social world. It is these kinds of questions which, in my view, need to be at the heart of the practice of integrating methods, if such a practice is to be successful. In particular, I think it is possible to identify three forms of questions which qualitative researchers get used to asking themselves, and which make a significant contribution to debates about integrating methods.

- The first question concerns the *purpose of integration* of methods. As I have argued throughout, qualitative researchers should ask themselves why they wish to combine methods, and there is potentially a wide range of answers to this question (see Chapters 2 and 4 in particular). However, asking the question at all means that the researcher is engaging in some useful self-interrogation about which parts of their intellectual puzzle, or which of their research questions, might be addressed by different methods, and how that might be done. In other words, by asking the question one is assuming from the start that the answer *may not* be straightforwardly that all the methods address the same parts of the intellectual puzzle. So, for example, the different methods may address specific parts of the puzzle, they may do it in distinctive ways (for example by tapping into various ontological levels of social reality), or approach the puzzle from diverse angles, and so on. Even the apparently simple answer that different methods address the same parts of the puzzle but in varying levels of detail (classically, that 'quantitative' methods provide breadth, and 'qualitative' methods provide depth), becomes less straightforward when one is forced to consider just what kind of social reality alternative methods assume is meaningful (see Chapters 3 and 4), and which parts of one's intellectual puzzle are actually accessible, epistemologically speaking, by particular data generation methods (see Chapter 2).

- The second question concerns the *mode of integration* of methods. Once a qualitative researcher is convinced that they know why they wish to combine methods, and that the combination they are planning is meaningful in relation to their research questions and intellectual puzzle, they will need to think carefully about how the integration is to be achieved. As I have argued, this involves working out whether the ontologies and epistemologies expressed in the different methods are complementary, as well as whether they can be made to be consistent in a technical sense. So, for example, if one method tells you about apples, and another tells you about pears, you have to first work out whether your intellectual puzzle is meaningfully addressed by explanations based on apples and pears, and then to determine exactly whether and how you can knit together your 'measurements' or analyses of the apples with those of the pears. Again, the habit of self-interrogation on such issues means that qualitative researchers are unlikely to begin with the less than helpful assumption that integration can be achieved unproblematically and will, instead, more usefully find themselves engaging in a situated and contextual way with the logistics of integration of particular methods in relation to particular research questions and puzzles. This is a practice which I think can usefully be adopted by all potential integrators of methods, whether or not they see themselves as being situated to one side or the other of a qualitative–quantitative divide.

- The third question concerns the *basis on which generalizations can be made* from one's research, which is a key question for anyone who is integrating methods. It is important to think through questions about whether different methods imply or support different forms of generalization and, if so, how they can be most meaningfully and usefully integrated. As I suggested in Chapter 7, there are more clearly established conventions for generalizing from quantitative than from qualitative data analyses. This, together with the undoubtedly more widespread public and political belief in the legitimacy and generalizability of quantitative analysis, has tended to mean that the methods by which qualitative researchers might generalize from their research have been subject to a great deal of critical scrutiny (see Finch, 1986; Hammersley, 1992; Schofield, 1993). This is, of course, no bad thing, and it is certainly the case that the early development of qualitative methods was characterized by an imbalance between too great a concern with how to generate qualitative data, and too little with how to analyse them and make generalizations in a systematic and convincing fashion. As a consequence of all this, qualitative researchers have had to ask themselves some very difficult questions about the basis on which they can make generalizations, and the role of validity and reliability of method in the process (see Chapters 5 and 7). However, I think that what we should learn from this is that these difficult questions need to be asked about *any* form of generalization, whether it is based on what are seen as qualitative or quantitative methods and analyses. So, for example, we must resist the assumption that generalization is unproblematic if it is defined as empirical generalization, and based upon analysis of data generated from a sample representative (in terms of surface characteristics) of a wider population. The difficult questions about validity of method and interpretation, about theoretical generalization, and about the logic by which explanations to intellectual puzzles are constructed and sustained, still apply in this example, and are not straightforwardly dealt with by the claim that the sample is representative in terms of selected variables. In making these points I am not seeking to criticize quantitative methods so much as to suggest that these questions must be asked about generalization from *any* method and *any* analysis, and they must be resolved before the integration of methods can be achieved. The specific nature of qualitative research as practised by the kinds of thinking, reflexive practitioners I have identified, and the socio-political context in which such research is done, mean in my view that the most interesting and important contributions to debates about the generalizability of *any* research in this context have come predominantly out of this stable.

I should reiterate that I am not suggesting that qualitative researchers have the monopoly on good ideas about integrating methods any more than they do on ethical and politically aware research practice. However, what I am saying is that qualitative researchers who ask themselves difficult questions, as I have advocated, are more likely (than qualitative researchers who do not, or quantitative researchers who have not had to) to find themselves up against the right kinds of questions with regard to integrating methods. They have arguably become more used to questioning the logic of their own epistemology, ontology, and research practice, and to defending their explanations and generalizations in the face of critical scrutiny. Some qualitative researchers will conclude that integration of method is not possible across what they see as an impenetrable qualitative–quantitative divide, others will say that there is no such divide, and still others will reject the very idea of being labelled *either* a qualitative *or* a quantitative researcher (for different views see Brannen, 1992; Bryman and Burgess, 1994; Fielding and Fielding, 1986; Hammersley, 1992). I have retained the working notion of a divide because I think it is suggestive of some differences in ontology and, more particularly, in epistemology and method. Also, I think it is easier to 'unlearn' some of the less than useful ideas about a divide (for example that integration within either side is unproblematic, but integration across it is impossible), than it is to move away from the erroneous idea that all forms of data and analyses are essentially the same. For example, cross-sectional variable analysis *should* be distinguished from holistic forms of analysis (see Chapters 5, 6 and 7), yet once the idea of variable analysis has taken hold in one's mind as *the* method of data analysis, it can become very difficult to conceptualize other possibilities. However, if we do retain some notion of a qualitative–quantitative divide in this way, I think it is important that we do not mystify it, or indeed reify it. As I have tried to emphasize, it is much more important and useful to ask ourselves difficult questions about all methods, than to assume their unproblematic location on one side or another of such a divide.

CONCLUSION

In this chapter I have sought to highlight some more general uses of the critical, thinking and reflexive research practice which I have advocated throughout the book. As well as representing, in my view, the best way to do qualitative research, I think that such a practice produces qualitative research *practitioners* who have important contributions to make to general debates about research and method in the social sciences. I selected two such debates for discussion in this chapter: ethics and politics on the one hand, and the integration of methods on the other. Both of these debates continue to be topical as well as long running, and have made clear gains from the inputs of qualitative researchers.

I began the book by saying that my aim was to make qualitative research seem possible in the eyes of would-be researchers, and to provide them with a set of tools and a mode of critical thinking to help them to do it. My focus on difficult questions which should and *can* be resolved was intended to provide access to these tools and modes of thinking, whilst also showing that qualitative research can be interesting, challenging and important. I am aware that the qualitative research practitioners created by all of this difficult questioning are likely to be people who, at each point in the research process, will be asking 'why?', 'how?', 'what are the consequences?', and producing for themselves a constant echo of 'yes, but it's not as simple as that'. This self-interrogation is the best way I can think of to go about producing qualitative research which is intellectually sophisticated, ethically and politically acceptable, practically feasible, socially relevant, as well as enjoyable and stimulating for those involved at all levels in creating and consuming it. I hope that it *does* make qualitative research seem possible, although the reader must, of course, be the final judge of that. Please do remember, though, when making your judgement, that I never said it would be easy.

REFERENCES

Ball, M.S. and Smith, G.W.H. (1992) *Analyzing Visual Data*, London: Sage

Bertaux, D. and Bertaux-Wiame, I. (1981) 'Life Stories in the Bakers' Trade' in D. Bertaux (ed.) *Biography and Society: the Life History Approach in the Social Sciences*, London: Sage

Blaikie, N. (1993) *Approaches to Social Enquiry*, Cambridge: Polity

Blumer, H. (1956) 'Sociological Analysis and the "Variable"' *American Sociological Review*, vol. 21, pp. 683–90

Blumer, H. (1969) *Symbolic Interactionism: Perspective and Method*, New Jersey: Prentice Hall

Brannen, J. (ed.) (1992) *Mixing Methods: Qualitative and Quantitative Research*, Aldershot: Avebury

Brewer, J. and Hunter A. (1989) *Multimethod Research: a Synthesis of Styles*, London: Sage

Bryman, A. (1988) *Quantity and Quality in Social Research*, London: Unwin Hyman

Bryman, A. and Burgess, R.G. (eds) (1994) *Analyzing Qualitative Data*, London: Routledge

Bryman, A. and Cramer, D. (1990) *Quantitative Analysis for Social Scientists*, London: Routledge

Bulmer, M. (ed.) (1982) *Social Research Ethics*, New York: Holmes and Meier

Burgess, R.G. (1982) *Field Research: a Sourcebook and Field Manual*, London: Allen and Unwin

Burgess, R.G. (1984) *In the Field: an Introduction to Field Research*, London: Allen and Unwin

Burgess, R.G. (ed.) (1986) *Key Variables in Social Investigation*, London: Routledge

Cicourel, A. (1964) *Method and Measurement in Sociology*, London: Free Press

Denzin, N.K. (1989) *The Research Act: a Theoretical Introduction to Sociological Methods* 3rd edn, New Jersey: Prentice Hall

Dey, I. (1993) *Qualitative Data Analysis: a User-Friendly Guide for Social Scientists*, London: Routledge

Dickens, D. and Fontana, A. (1994) *Postmodernism and Social Inquiry*, London: UCL Press

Fairclough, N. (1992) *Discourse and Social Change*, Cambridge: Polity

Fielding, N.G. and Fielding, J.L. (1986) *Linking Data*, London: Sage

Fielding, N.G. and Lee, R.M. (eds) (1991) *Using Computers in Qualitative Research*, London: Sage

Finch, J. (1984) '"It's Great To Have Someone to Talk To": Ethics and Politics of Interviewing Women' in C. Bell and H. Roberts (eds) *Social Researching: Politics, Problems, Practice*, London: Routledge

Finch, J. (1986) *Research and Policy: the Uses of Qualitative Methods in Social and Educational Research*, London: Falmer

Finch, J. and Mason, J. (1990) 'Decision Taking in the Fieldwork Process: Theoretical Sampling and Collaborative Working' in R.G. Burgess (ed.) *Studies in Qualitative Methodology*, vol. 2, JAI Press, pp. 25–50

Garfinkel, H. (1967) *Studies in Ethnomethodology*, New Jersey: Prentice Hall

Glaser, B.G. and Strauss, A.L. (1967) *The Discovery of Grounded Theory*, Chicago: Aldine

Hammersley, M. (1992) *What's Wrong with Ethnography?*, London: Routledge

Hammersley, M. (1995) *The Politics of Social Research*, London: Sage

Hammersley, M. and Atkinson, P. (1995) *Ethnography: Principles in Practice*, 2nd edn, London: Routledge

Haraway, D. (1988) 'Situated Knowledges: the Science Question in Feminism and the Privilege of the Partial Perspective' *Feminist Studies*, vol. 14, no. 3, pp. 573–99

Harding, S. (1986) *The Science Question in Feminism*, Milton Keynes: Open University Press

Hareven, T.K. (1982) *Family Time and Industrial Time*, Cambridge: Cambridge University Press

Harper, D. (1994) 'On the Authority of the Image: Visual Methods at the Crossroads', in N.K. Denzin and Y.S. Lincoln (eds) *Handbook of Qualitative Research*, London: Sage

Henriques, J., Hollway, W., Urwin, C., Venn, C. and Walkerdine, V. (1984) *Changing the Subject: Psychology, Social Regulation and Subjectivity*, London: Methuen

Henwood, K.L. and Pidgeon, N.F. (1992) 'Qualitative Research and Psychological Theorizing' *British Journal of Psychology*, vol. 83, pp. 97–111

Hockings, P. (ed.) (1975) *Principles of Visual Anthropology*, Mouton

Hodder, I. (1994) 'The Interpretation of Documents and Material Culture' in N.K. Denzin and Y.S. Lincoln (eds) *Handbook of Qualitative Research*, London: Sage

Holland, J. and Ramazanoglu, C. (1994) 'Coming to Conclusions: Power and Interpretation in Researching Young Women's Sexuality' in M. Maynard and J. Purvis (eds) *Researching Women's Lives from a Feminist Perspective*, London: Taylor and Francis

Hollway, W. (1989) *Subjectivity and Method in Psychology: Gender, Meaning and Science*, London: Sage

Homan, R. (1991) *The Ethics of Social Research*, London: Longman

Hughes, J. (1990) *The Philosophy of Social Research*, 2nd edn, London: Longman

Mason, J. (1994) 'Linking Qualitative and Quantitative Data Analysis' in A. Bryman and R.G. Burgess (eds) *Analyzing Qualitative Data*, London: Routledge

Maynard, M. (1994) 'Methods, Practice and Epistemology: the Debate about Feminism and Research' in M. Maynard and J. Purvis (eds) *Researching Women's Lives from a Feminist Perspective*, London: Taylor and Francis

Maynard, M. and Purvis, J. (eds) (1994) *Researching Women's Lives from a Feminist Perspective*, London: Taylor and Francis

Miles, M.B. and Huberman, A.M. (1994) *Qualitative Data Analysis: an Expanded Sourcebook*, 2nd edn, London: Sage

Oliver, M. (1992) 'Changing the Social Relations of Research Production?' *Disability, Handicap and Society*, vol. 7, no. 2, pp. 101–14

Patton, M. (1987) *How to use Qualitative Methods in Evaluation*, London: Sage

Pawson, R. (1989) *A Measure for Measures: a Manifesto for Empirical Sociology*, London: Routledge

Platt, J. (1981) 'Evidence and Proof in Documentary Research' *Sociological Review*, vol. 29, no. 1, pp. 31–66

Platt, J. (1988) 'What Can Case Studies Do?' in R.G. Burgess (ed.) *Studies in Qualitative Methodology*, vol. 1, JAI Press, pp. 1–23

Plummer, K. (1983) *Documents of Life: an Introduction to the Problems and Literature of a Humanistic Method*, London: Allen and Unwin

Potter, J. and Wetherell, M. (1987) *Discourse and Social Psychology*, London: Sage

Rose, H. (1994) *Love, Power and Knowledge: towards a Feminist Transformation of the Sciences*, Cambridge: Polity

Ruby, J. (ed.) (1989) *Visual Anthropology*, London: Harwood Academic

Schofield, J.W. (1993) 'Increasing the Generalizability of Qualitative Research' in M. Hammersley (ed.) *Social Research: Philosophy, Politics and Practice*, London: Sage

Schutz, A. (1976) *The Phenomenology of the Social World*, London: Heinemann

Scott, J. (1990) *A Matter of Record: Documentary Sources in Social Research*, Cambridge: Polity

Silverman, D. (1993) *Interpreting Qualitative Data: Methods for Analysing Talk, Text and Interaction*, London: Sage

Skeggs, B. (1994) 'Situating the Production of Feminist Ethnography' in M. Maynard and J. Purvis (eds) *Researching Women's Lives from a Feminist Perspective*, London: Taylor and Francis

Smith, D. (1988) *The Everyday World as Problematic: a Feminist Sociology*, Milton Keynes: Open University Press

Stanley, L. and Wise, S. (1993) *Breaking Out Again: Feminist Ontology and Epistemology*, London: Routledge

Strauss, A. (1987) *Qualitative Analysis for Social Scientists*, Cambridge: Cambridge University Press

Strauss, A. and Corbin, J. (1990) *Basics of Qualitative Research: Grounded Theory Procedures and Techniques*, London: Sage

Tesch, R. (1990) *Qualitative Research: Analysis Types and Software Tools*, London: Falmer

Yin, R.K. (1989) *Case Study Research: Design and Methods*, London: Sage

Index